THE F***KET LIST

Things I Will NOT Be Doing Before I Die

David M. Stameshkin

ISBN-10: 0989394204
ISBN-13: 9780989394208

For Anne and Elizabeth
And all my students

Table of Contents

Preface

S o, what's a "F**ket List"? As I approached retirement
recently from Franklin & Marshall College in Lancaster,
Pennsylvania, where I worked as an administrator and
occasional history professor for 34 years, I noticed that just
about everyone else in the world seemed to be preparing
a "Bucket List," i.e., a compilation of all the things that they
wanted to do before they died. I thought I should probably
have a Bucket List, too, but as I started working on mine,
I realized that there were at least as many things I was certain
I did *not* want to do (or knew I couldn't do) as there were
things I wanted to do and could possibly accomplish. So, in
addition to making a Bucket List, I started making a F**ket
List, i.e., the things I am *not* going to do before I die—the
things about which I would just say: "F**k it, there's no way
I can and/or want to do that."

Since I was 67, and right on the leading edge of the so-called
Baby Boomers, I thought it might be helpful to the millions of
Boomers retiring right behind me to see an example of a F**ket
List, in addition to all those Bucket Lists out there. As I started
thinking about my list, I found myself trying to explain why
I might have wanted to do something at one point in my life

and why I didn't want to do it now. This caused my initial short list to grow into a manuscript that reads suspiciously at times like a memoir. I should apologize for that, but since apparently just about everyone is writing a memoir these days (as well as a Bucket List), I don't feel too guilty.

Many people reluctantly give up some of their most cherished dreams early in their lives; however, as retirement approaches, they sometimes start to think about pursuing those old ambitions and/or "reinventing themselves" now that they may have time and the financial means to do so. When I was a little boy, I wanted to follow in my father's footsteps and become a great salesman. As a teenager, I wanted to be a Rabbi, or a stand-up comic. I also spent two summers while going through college driving a cab in Chicago, and during my graduate school days (when it looked sometimes as if I would never find a permanent place in academe), I thought occasionally of taxi driving as a career.

As I began to make my Bucket List and thought carefully about all of these roads not taken, I reminisced about why I had seriously considered them as career options, and asked myself if I wanted to pick up one or more of these discarded careers and try again. In each case, as I relate through the stories that follow, I reluctantly (or not so reluctantly) placed them on my F**ket List. So that's what the book is about, and I am hopeful you will enjoy these stories.

Some of the names of people and companies in these stories have been changed or omitted to reduce the likelihood that I will be sued successfully. The stories, however, are true—at least this is the way I remember them!

NOTE: People who have read this manuscript before publication have told me that, while all the chapters are funny and interesting, the second chapter (stories about my cab driving experiences in Chicago) were particularly enjoyable. So, if you just want to sample things in this book, turn to Chapter 2. But, in any case, please don't give up on the book until you have read Chapter 2. I promise you that after reading those stories, if you don't feel that you have received your money's worth, contact me, and I will send you…a sincere apology!

There are many people who have assisted me in this project. In particular, Anne Stameshkin, Elizabeth Stameshkin, Lee and Esther Erman, Sandy Asher, and Sheila Bihary have offered helpful advice for which I am very grateful. Dane Low of Ebook Launch not only designed the cover, but kindly answered many questions I had about publishing. I especially want to thank my wife, Colleen, who has had to listen to these stories too many times over the 44 years we have been married, and who has kindly reminded me not to embellish (too much). The book is dedicated to my two daughters, Anne and Elizabeth, whom I hope will consider passing them on to future generations, and to all my students who have laughed at these stories over the past 44 years and urged me to write them down. Well, guys, here they are!

David M. Stameshkin
Lancaster, Pennsylvania
April 26, 2013

Chapter 1:

WHY I'M NOT GOING TO BE A SALESMAN

"Son, when you finish talking with people, if they don't feel better, happier, or more informed, you have failed in your conversation. If you succeed, people will always want to see you again."

—Sam Stameshkin, The Greatest Salesman in the World

The Greatest Salesman in the World

MY FATHER, SAM STAMESHKIN, was The Greatest Salesman in the World. I know that because, when I was in grade school in the 1950s, I used to accompany him occasionally in the summers when he sold Rusco aluminum and steel combination storm and screen windows to residential customers all over St. Paul, Minnesota. He could sell anything to anyone. Earlier in his life he sold insurance for Prudential (he told me he held sales records with Prudential in the Midwest); and he sold goods from a bakery truck (I still remember the wonderful mixed smell of baked goods and gasoline that suffused the Tassies Bakery garage on St. Clair Street in St. Paul).

But through most of the 1950s, he sold windows. And he sold them to all kinds of people: rich and poor, old and young, black and white, men and women. He really knew how to deal with people. Without ever being hypocritical, he knew how to make them feel good about themselves. He knew how to entertain people with his stories, his songs, and his wonderful laugh. And he knew whom to bring along to help him with a sale. If his customers were elderly, he brought his mother—my grandmother, Jennie; if they loved dogs, he brought our crazy Irish Setter, Kelly; and if they liked little kids, he brought me.

I loved the summer evenings when Sam Stameshkin, The Greatest Salesman in the World, told me that the next morning he would need me to help him sell windows. We would enter the customers' house the next day, and my father would win their hearts within minutes. What a charmer. They loved him! He let me help him prepare the estimates. He would measure the windows and read off the measurements to me, and I would write them down in his official estimates book. I could do math in my head from an early age, so I would quickly figure out the estimated cost of everything. This caused a small sensation every time I did it, and my father glowed in the admiration I received from his customers.

"Sam, you've got a little genius on your hands!"

"He's a big help to me."

I would always thank the people, and quickly add in my high-pitched nerdy little-boy voice: "You should really consider buying Rusco Windows—the Cadillac of windows—because my father says they are the best combination storm and screen windows on the market—particularly the ones made of hot-dipped galvanized steel—and my father never lies to me. In fact, my father told me that if I ever became a salesman, I absolutely had to believe in the product or I should get out of the business. My father would never sell anything he didn't believe in."

The customers enjoyed this speech coming from a tiny eight-year-old. "Sam, you've got a chip off the old block here! You've taught him well. Some day, he might be able to be a better salesman than you."

"No!" I'd interrupt, horrified. "Nobody will ever be a better salesman than my father. Sam Stameshkin is the Greatest Salesman in the World." Before long, the customers were signing a contract with my father.

He had so many satisfied customers that, after a sale, he could always stop at a nearby home just to ask how the windows were working out. The very satisfied former customers would break into huge smiles when they saw my father coming. We would always be offered coffee and something sweet, and my father was introduced to more neighbors who were nearby, resulting often in more potential customers.

After one of these visits, I mentioned how happy people always were to see him.

He replied, "Son, when you finish talking with people, if they don't feel better, happier, or more informed, you have failed in your conversation. If you succeed, people will always want to see you again." I've never forgotten that, and I've tried, as much as possible, to live my life by that rule.

Every year in November, my father would give me a list of the names and addresses of hundreds of his former customers, along with hundreds of Christmas cards. I addressed and stamped the envelopes and enclosed the cards on which he had written kind personal messages. I'm sure that this nice little

Jewish boy sent out more Christmas cards each year than all the Christian kids in my elementary school class combined! While I was working on the cards, I dreamed that someday I would be a great salesman like my father, and that people would smile and look happy when they saw me coming.

The Wrong Side of the Street

My father and mother separated when I was 14, and my father died two years later. Soon after they separated, my mother's employer, the North Central Association of Colleges and Secondary Schools (an agency that accredits all the high schools and colleges in the Midwest) decided to move its headquarters from the University of Minnesota to the University of Chicago. To keep her executive position, my mother and I moved from St. Paul to Chicago in the summer of 1960.

I wanted to go away to college when I graduated from high school in 1963, but my mother—by dint of subtle persuasion and a few tears ("I'll be all alone, but that's okay") that left me with enormous feelings of guilt—convinced me to forget my desire to attend Harvard or Yale, and to stay in Chicago instead and enroll at the University of Chicago. Since I had been granted a four-year full tuition scholarship to Chicago, I at least won her approval (after much begging and pleading) to live in the dorms, about 15 minutes from her apartment. We still saw each other a lot. I brought home my laundry, had at least one meal a week there, and often borrowed the car for dates. We even participated in a "husband-wife" bowling league sponsored by our synagogue on Monday nights during my freshman year. My college friends ribbed me unmercifully about that. And it got worse: my mother started to date the faculty head of house in Shorey House, where I lived. Every Saturday night, this geology professor used to bring her back to his apartment, just down the hall from my room. As soon as his door shut, the guys were relentless in their kidding. "Hey, David, you're mom's doing better than you!" Really hilarious.

From the time I was 16, my mother had arranged for me to work in her office as a clerk every summer. It was fairly easy work, the office was air-conditioned, and I made about $70 a week, but I was eager to try something more challenging—and something where my mother wasn't my boss.

My opportunity to try something new appeared in the summer of 1963, when I had just graduated from high school. I saw an ad for a job that really excited me, and I signed up to become a summer management trainee in encyclopedia sales. This was my big chance to see if I had my father's genius for sales! The job advertisement promised a salary of $125 a week, even if you didn't sell anything. That was a princely sum in those days for summer work: for example, beginning teachers earned about the same salary—only about $6,000 a year. The company also promised that you would only make calls at homes where the people had asked for a salesperson to come. It sounded great. Only later did I learn that you worked entirely on commission ($81 for every sale), and it was door-to-door cold turkey sales.

I began my career in encyclopedia sales with three days of intensive training, during which I learned a 45-minute sales presentation by heart. The pitch (in abridged form) went something like this: "Hi, I'm David Stameshkin, I'm doing some work in this area talking to everybody. Do you mind if I step in and ask you a few questions. The reason we call in the evening is to get the wife and husband together. Can you get your wife

5

in here for a minute? I'm with the Enlightenment Company. How would you like to have in your home absolutely free our new 24-volume picture encyclopedia? What's the catch? After you've had this great encyclopedia in your home for six months, I am going to come back and ask you how you liked it. I will ask you to give me an honest appraisal (I think you will be ecstatic), and the company will ask you to let us tell all your neighbors how much you liked it. With your endorsement, we think we can sell your neighbors our product. So you get a free encyclopedia, and we make a lot of money."

Of course, it wasn't really free. The customer had to agree to buy the yearbook for the next ten years and a bookcase to put it in, and a few other things. By the time they were done, they were paying about $.20 a day for the rest of their natural lives ("a dime a day for the morning paper and a quarter on Sunday for the Sunday funnies" was our spiel).

The training session began each morning with a one-hour motivational class, after which we learned and perfected our sales pitch. Our trainer, Fred Jones, was a former football player, coach, and sports announcer who had allegedly been thrown out of his radio job for swearing on the air. He was about 40 years old, 6'3" and weighed 230 pounds. He wore a tee shirt, athletic shorts, and gym shoes; he looked like he was about to start calisthenics drills. He even had a whistle. He sat on an exercise bike in front of the room, with his prominent leg muscles exposed as he screamed at his thirty youthful charges.

"You are King's Men! Do you hear me? Say 'King's Men!'"

"King's Men!"

"I can't hear you!"

"KING'S MEN"

"LOUDER!"

6

"KING'S MEN!"

"Now you'll do whatever I say, right?"

"RIGHT"

"Take off your pants!" We all dropped our pants.

"Put your pants on, you look stupid."

"Yessir," we quickly complied.

"And there's nothing you can't do if you want it bad enough! You (pointing to me)! Run through that door." He pointed to a door at the front of the room behind him. I ran as hard as I could into the door, slamming my toes and elbows into the door to make a loud noise, throwing my head back to look as if I had smashed my head into the door, and fell to the floor. It was a great act. He loved it.

"Now THAT'S the King's Men spirit. Good!"

Fred taught us the King's Men Handshake: As you grab the hand of the other person, you rotate their hand below yours. "That way," he sneered, "you both know who's on top!"

Fred also made us memorize the names of all the highest-ranking officers of the Company, including "Fat" Frank Fritzhammer, the 315-pound Vice President of Operations.

Fred was a great motivator: Indeed, all of us were highly motivated to learn the 45-minute speech as fast as possible to get out of his morning sessions. In three days, I was declared ready for the road. My manager dropped me in Morton Grove, a northern Chicago suburb at 2 p.m., and said he would pick me up at 9 p.m. It began to rain, and continued incessantly for the next six hours. I did not have a coat. The endless suburban housing tract to which I had been assigned had no restaurants or public rest rooms—just one house after another. Nobody let me in, my charming demeanor notwithstanding. And by 7 p.m., I was wet, hungry, dying to take a leak, and greatly discouraged. But I kept on going until my manager picked me up at 9 p.m.

The next day, it was sunny, and I rejoined the effort with renewed enthusiasm. After all, I only needed to place one set ($81 commission) to surpass my former weekly salary ($70) at my mother's office. At the third house, the man was very pleasant. We talked for quite a while, and he told me to come back in 30 minutes when his wife was scheduled to return from shopping (we had to have the wife and husband together when we made our pitch). I came back, and the man said that he had called the local police station, and I was not registered to sell in the town. I told him that my manager *had* registered us in Morton Grove. His mouth tightened, and he pointed across the street.

"*That's* Morton Grove. *This* is Glenview. I'm the Glenview volunteer police chief, and you're under arrest. We don't allow people like you in *Glenview*." He showed me his badge, and escorted me to a downstairs bedroom. On one hand, things looked bad; on the other hand, after two days, I had finally gained entrance into someone's house! The man pointed to a chair in the corner of the room furthest from the door.

"Sit down, and a policeman will be here to take you down to the station. While you're waiting, I'll put on some music for you. What do you like?" He had a beautiful quadraphonic sound system.

"I like classical."

"Hmm. I don't have much of that." He opened up his cabinets. There were about one zillion country-and-western albums, and one classical record—*Maria Callas' Greatest Hits*. He put it on full blast and locked the doors. I tried to tell him that the only kind of classical music I *didn't* like was sopranos singing opera, but it was too late. Years later, when I saw the Stanley Kubrick film classic, *A Clockwork Orange*, in which the authorities try to use Beethoven recordings to modify the behavior of the sadistic anti-hero protagonist, I felt great sympathy for that creep. I prayed the police would come before Maria, blasting through four speakers, drove me insane. Gradually, Maria's voice began to compete with a siren of some kind. The door opened suddenly, and a burly policeman with his gun drawn burst into the room. I jumped up and threw my hands into the air.

"Don't shoot—I'm just selling encyclopedias."

"All right, assume the position."

"Sir?"

"Hands against the wall, and spread those legs." He frisked me. "Hands behind your back." He put handcuffs on me.

"Is this necessary? I'm just selling encyclopedias, sir!"

The police chief responded. "We want your kind to know how you'll be treated if you try to upset the good people of Glenview. We're going to make an example of you, son."

They led me outside. The police siren had caused quite a crowd to form. They saw me coming out handcuffed, and there was a buzz. They probably thought I had murdered somebody. Admittedly, I *had* wanted to kill Maria Callas.

The police officer took me down to the station and took my cuffs off. He let me have my one phone call, and I informed the downtown office what had happened. They said they would send somebody there as soon as possible to get me out. The officer started to type my bond notice. He was doing it painfully, one letter at a time in the slowest hunt-and-peck style I had ever seen. I offered to do it for him. He looked at me incredulously. I told him I typed 75 words a minute, and that before I had embarked on my career of crime, I had been a secretary in a legitimate organization. After much thought, he reluctantly agreed. As I typed the bond notice, I saw him looking through my sales kit.

"Is this a good encyclopedia?" he asked.

"You bet. Were you thinking of buying one?"

"Yeah, the wife was talking about it last week. We have three kids in school, and she thought it would be a big help."

I completed my typing, and handed him the finished product. He looked it over, and seemed genuinely pleased. Feeling the moment was right, I launched into my sales pitch. After about ten minutes, just as I thought I finally had him really interested, a huge man came into the office. I immediately recognized him.

"Why you're Fat Frank Fritzhammer, Vice President for Operations."

"Good memory, young man. I happen to live in Glenview, and I'm on vacation. When the downtown office called me to let me know what had happened, I volunteered to get you out." He put out his hand to shake mine, and I tried to negotiate the King's Men Handshake, only to have Fat Frank easily rotate on top of me and just about break my relatively small hand. "Ha Ha Ha! Didn't they tell you that I invented that handshake? Nobody outshakes Fat Frank Fritzhammer! Let's get you out of here."

I whispered to him, "I'm about to place an order with this guy."

"Where's his wife, Dave? You can't sell without the wife—YOU know that! First rule! Come on, let's get out of here." He paid some money to the officer, and I reluctantly left without a sale. I never did sell a set. What a failure. The only good thing about my arrest was that the company used my case to challenge the blue law that required companies to register before selling door-to-door. I only had to appear once several weeks later in Glenview and plead not guilty. After that, the corporation's lawyers handled everything. I heard that my case eventually went to the Illinois Supreme Court where the law and my conviction were apparently overturned.

That night I went home and recounted my experiences to my mother. She was a lot angrier than I thought she would be, and she refused to let me continue working for the company. Fred Jones, my motivator, tried to convince my mother on the telephone the next morning to change her mind. Unfortunately, the sleazy assistant coach lost out to the emancipated Victorian Socialist Jewish mother.

"Now, little mother," he intoned, "you've got to let your boy loose from those apron strings. Hey, he's not in jail any more!"

"Listen you creep, my kid's been in sit-ins and demonstrations and I never disapproved. At least in those cases, if he were arrested, it would be for a good purpose. But to go to jail because he is involved in your sleazy bait-and-switch operation—forget it! " She hung up, and that was it. I could see Fred fuming while he churned even harder on his exercise bike.

The next day, I reluctantly went back to working for my mother. I figured my father's sales genes had bypassed me. On the other hand, I was sure my father—The Greatest Salesman in the World—was looking down from heaven not with a sad frown, but rather with a big smile. I can almost hear him now: "Don't despair! David, my boy, go back to that Glenview police officer and close that sale. You almost had it! You can do this. My God, you almost sold a set to the guy who's trying to put you in jail!" He was The Greatest Salesman in the World, in part, because he never gave up. So I kept that career path window open just a crack.

The Car Salesman

I entered the University of Chicago that fall, and, after thinking seriously about law school for a number of years, I walked out of my LSAT exam in my senior year. Instead, impressed with the brilliance and erudition of my U. of C. professors, I decided to follow in their footsteps and become an academic. I obtained a Master's Degree at the University of Wisconsin-Madison and a Ph.D. from the University of Michigan-Ann Arbor in history, and began a long and moderately successful career in college teaching and administration. My mother passed away in 1972, while I was studying at Michigan, so she knew I was pursuing a career that she valued, and she was very pleased. But I also had a chance to use my father's knowledge of people (and of sales) to perform my job and other tasks more effectively.

From the time we were married in 1968, my wife, Colleen, and I always owned at least one car and usually two. We would try to keep our cars eight years and then sell them before they started to fall apart. Given my excitement about sales, I was assigned the role of salesman. I always tried to keep my father's sales lessons in mind; in particular, I tried to tell the truth about the cars I was selling. This led to some rather unexpected consequences.

We purchased our first car, a lightly used Austin America, shortly after we were married in June of 1968. It had been highly recommended by *Consumer Reports*. This import had a transverse engine, and very few mechanics knew how to work on it. This wasn't a problem until the summer of 1971. Arthur (that's what we named the car) was overheating. We tried numerous mechanics, but none of them could figure it out. We were living in Philadelphia, where I was working on a potential doctoral dissertation project, but we had to get back to Ann Arbor where my wife was scheduled to teach for the fall semester. Arthur overheated after about 100 miles on the Pennsylvania Turnpike. We stopped at a service area, put in fresh water, waited for the engine to cool down, and started up again. Arthur went about 75 miles, and we repeated the process. Each time, he was able to go fewer and fewer miles without overheating. Eventually, as we were just trying to make it from one oasis to the next on the Ohio Turnpike, Arthur died halfway between two service areas. It was night by that time, and there we were—Colleen, Isaac (our cat), and I—stuck on the side of the Ohio Turnpike 20 miles east of the Fremont exit, praying that a state police car or some kind driver would stop and help us. There were no cell phones in 1971.

Suddenly, a pickup truck backed up to our car. A tall, gangly young man came up to our window, and said: "Hi, I'm Greg Johnson. I'm not a mechanic, but maybe I can help?" We told him our sad tale, and he said that he could tow us to the next service area because he had a chain in his truck. We gratefully agreed, and he attached the short chain from the back of his truck to the front of Arthur. He told me that I needed to steer and use the brakes because if he broke quickly, Arthur (and all of us) would crash into the back of the truck. Greg started up the truck and we started to move. I was petrified that Greg was going to have to brake suddenly, and that would be the end of all of us! We went 20 miles to the service area, with my eyes glued to his rear brake lights, and my hands glued to the steering wheel. It took all of Colleen's strength to remove my hands from the wheel when Greg finally pulled us into the service area.

The mechanics had all gone home for the night, and they wouldn't be back until the next day. Greg asked us if we would like to leave the car and ride with him to Ann Arbor. He was on his way to another college in Michigan for fraternity rush, and he would be going right by Ann Arbor. We jumped at the opportunity. We loaded everything in his pickup truck, including Isaac, and off we went.

It was quite a trip. It turned out that whenever there was a car on the side of the road, Greg would slow down, back up, and approach the driver of the car. "Hi, I'm Greg Johnson. I'm not a mechanic, but maybe I can help?" One car contained two young people making love (that was a little awkward), but the others actually had problems with their cars. So, we spent quite a bit of time that night helping stranded motorists. I even ended up lending money to one couple. It took a long time to travel the 100 miles from the service area on the Ohio Turnpike to Ann Arbor, but it was a good feeling to help many others and still get home.

I found a company that would tow Arthur, and once we had him back in Ann Arbor, I took him to the dealer. They quickly determined that it was just a broken thermostat, and, although Arthur's engine casing looked like it had been set on fire at some point, the car seemed to work. The dealer told us that given what the car had been through, it might be better to just use it around town.

My mother became quite ill that fall, and we were told she was probably going to die of cancer sometime in the spring. She had just bought a new Chevy Nova to replace her old Rambler before she realized how sick she was. She had given me the Rambler, which was old, but in somewhat better shape than Arthur, and we decided to sell Arthur. The first buyer came to our apartment, and, following my father's advice to always tell the truth about your product, I immediately started to tell the potential buyer everything that had gone wrong on the trip home from Philadelphia. I opened the hood and showed him the blackened insides. I told him that the dealer had warned us to use it only as a town car and not chance going out on the interstate. I told him that most mechanics couldn't deal with the transverse engine, and that we weren't sure what other damage had been done to the car by the constant overheating. I must have gone on for quite a while, because the guy finally said, "Are you going to let me test drive this car or not?"

As we settled into Arthur, the guy told me he needed a car to commute from Ann Arbor to Detroit on I-94. I told him that he should probably get a different car. I noticed he was heading for the interstate, and I reiterated what I had said. He was completely ignoring me.

"Well, let's see how she runs at 70," he said.

"Sir, I really think this is a mistake. The dealer said…

"Yeah, yeah, I heard all that. But let's just see how she runs."

Pretty soon we were on the interstate going 80, and I was sure this would be my last ride.

"Yeah this baby runs fine," he said. "Let's see how she does at 90." I was too stupefied to answer. Eventually, he took an exit and we drove back to the house. We got out of the car. I kissed the ground quickly.

"So, you're asking $750 for this?"

"Sir, you don't want to buy this car. It just isn't in good enough shape to go 80-90 miles per hour every day on the interstate! Please reconsider."

"All right, I'll give you $800."

"No, I'm not trying to get you to give more money. I'm going to be feeling very guilty if something happens to you because you drive this car to Detroit on the interstate."

"Okay, $850, but not a dollar more." He got up to leave.

"All right, all right, I give up. You win. Take the car." We completed the paper work and he took Arthur. Colleen thought the whole transaction was very funny. She couldn't believe how unsuccessful I had been in convincing this guy not to buy the car. "I've never seen anybody try so hard NOT to sell something." She couldn't stop laughing.

"This is no laughing matter, dear! What if this guy dies on the interstate! I'm an accomplice!"

"David, I heard you warn him. You pointed out every single thing that is wrong with Arthur—twice or three times—you did fine." My wife's major field was ethics, and she once excoriated me for borrowing a knife and fork from the University of Wisconsin Union for my use during the school year (I was going to give them back—honest!). So, if she thought I had acted ethically, I shouldn't have worried any more. But I couldn't help myself. I checked the obituaries and traffic accidents in the *Ann Arbor News* every day for the next several months, certain that I would be reading about Arthur's owner. I saw nothing, but that did not reduce the huge guilt I felt as a likely accomplice in his future death.

My mother died in April 1972, just a few months after we sold Arthur. I inherited her almost-new Nova, and Colleen and I decided to sell the Rambler. Once again, I was designated as the salesman; after all, I'd sold Arthur to the first person who inquired. We had a quick response to our ad for the Rambler, and a young Pakistani graduate student couple with two little children came to our apartment to look at the car. The Rambler was about seven years old and not a very powerful car. As I had done with Arthur, I went down a long litany of things that were wrong with the car. The husband told us he wanted to pull a large U-Haul trailer across the Rocky Mountains to California, where he had just been hired to teach at one of the schools in the California State College system. I laughed and told him the Rambler could possibly make it over the Rockies, but *not* if it were pulling anything, much less a large U-Haul trailer with the furniture of a family of four. He persisted, and so did I.

"You are asking $450?"

"Yes."

"Okay, I will take it."

"But, sir, this car will die in the mountains, and there you will be with your family and all your goods and no way to get to California!"

"I will offer you $500."

"No, I don't want more money. I just don't want you to buy this car if you are going to cross the Rockies in it and pull a trailer."

"Okay. $550, but that's my last offer."

"No! No! You don't have to pay me more than the $450 we advertised. Okay, fine, I give! It's yours!" We did the paperwork, and he took the car away. Colleen was very pleased.

"You missed your calling, David. You are a born salesman."

"Are you kidding? Because my father told me to tell the truth about whatever I was selling, I go way overboard listing every little thing that's ever been wrong with the cars."

"But they love you for that. And then they trust you! Your father would be proud."

"Oh, yeah, right. That's why Arthur is going 90 miles an hour every day between Ann Arbor and Detroit, and the Rambler is about to pull a U-Haul 2,000 miles across the Rockies! "

But maybe she had a point. Over the next 25 years, I sold six more of our cars to private buyers, and every time it was to the first person who answered the ad. I used the same technique, and I reduced my guilt trip by being completely honest.

Finally, my streak came to an end in 2006, when my younger daughter, Elizabeth, asked me to sell her 2002 Ford Escort. It had originally been a rental car, and she purchased it in 2004 in Los Angeles, where she was between jobs after graduating from Caltech. Well, actually, she was unemployed and broke at the time, so my wife and I purchased it for $8,000. It turned out to be—in my daughter's words—"a horrific lemon," and that was one of the *nicest* things she ever said about it! The transmission died on her first attempt to drive it from Los Angeles to San Francisco. The good news was that the transmission was still under warranty; the bad news was that it took three weeks to repair. Not only that, the key often wouldn't turn the car on, and we would get an occasional frantic call. It turned out that this was also related to the problem with the transmission (the gear shift had to be perfectly engaged in Park for the car to start). Eventually, she drove it out to the University of Michigan in 2005, when she enrolled in the Law School. The check engine light came on that year and decided never to turn off again. She drove it to Lancaster, Pennsylvania, where my wife and I lived. We had just purchased a Prius, so we gave her our old car, and she asked us to sell the Escort for whatever we could get.

I was, of course, assigned again to sell the vehicle. I tried to get the check engine light fixed before I was going to sell it; the mechanic, however, said it had a short and he couldn't fix it, but not to worry since everything was fine with the engine. Well, I worry about everything, and so I wasn't happy; still, I had already put the ad in the paper, and before I could take it to another mechanic, the first person called to ask about the car. She wanted to see it immediately, so I reluctantly agreed, and she came over later that day.

I assumed that, given my past record with first customers, the car would be sold that day (even with a shining check engine light). The potential buyer arrived early in the evening. She was a very young Asian-American woman. I started, as usual, by listing all the things that had gone wrong with this car. She seemed impatient, and interrupted my tale of woe to ask if she could drive it. I said to go ahead, and she said she wanted me to come along. So she drove it around the neighborhood for about five minutes, and we returned to the house.

"I don't like the way it handles. When did you last have it realigned?"

"Well, I just had it looked over carefully by my mechanic, and he said the alignment was fine. On the other hand, I don't know why the check engine light won't go off, and neither does the mechanic. If you want to take it to another mechanic..."

"I heard a rattle in the back somewhere. It's pretty loud and annoying."

"Really? I haven't heard anything."

"It turns funny. How old are the tires?"

And the conversation continued like this for about ten minutes. She criticized every single aspect of the automobile. Finally, I said:

"Well, I guess you aren't interested in buying the car, but thanks for coming by."

"Wait, you are asking $4,000—correct? "

"Yes."

"I'll give you $3,000."

"Are you kidding? You just told me that it handled poorly, had bad tires, and rattled. You hate the color of the car and the interior makes you want to throw up. You said that brakes felt like they were going to stop working any minute, and that you are having trouble seeing out the back window. Why would you want to buy this car?

"All right. $3,400. But that's my final offer."

"Young lady. I'm not going to sell you this car for any amount of money. You hate this car! You should never buy anything you hate!"

"Okay, I'll give you $3,800. That's only $200 less than what you wanted."

"I don't think you are hearing me. I'm not selling this car to you. Good day." And I shut the door. She looked so befuddled. It later occurred to me that somebody probably told her to criticize the car, and then use those excuses to ask for a lower price. And then it hit me: I had not sold the car to the first customer! I had been so proud of that streak! When I told my wife what had happened, she said that the girl had offered to buy it—three times!—and so I could still say that the first customer always wanted to buy the car.

This reminded me of a joke I had heard. A very religious woman is trapped in her house by a sudden flood. She prayed to God to save her. A policeman came by in a rowboat and asked her to wade out of the house into the boat. The woman turned him down and said, "The Lord will provide." The waters kept rising and she moved up to the second floor. A large motor boat came to get her, but, again, she refused to leave, saying, "The Lord will provide." Finally the waters rose so high that she had to move up to the roof of her house. A helicopter came and hovered above the house. A man came down on the roof and started to put a harness on the woman to carry her up to the helicopter. "Come on, ma'am. Let me take you off the roof, or you are going to die." "No," she said, "The Lord will provide." Well, the helicopter left, and soon the woman drowned. She went to heaven, and when she met St. Peter at the pearly gates, she was angry. "I died in a flood. I thought God would save me." Suddenly, God's voice resounds at the gate. "Madam, I tried three times—I sent a row boat, a motor boat, and a helicopter. What more did you want from me?"

Not one other customer answered the ad, and I was forced to sell it to a dealer for $2,000. That's when I began to realize deep down that I was not cut out to be a salesman after all. My inadequacies were simple: too much concern for honesty and potential guilt, and not enough common sense and desire to close the deal.

The Admission Tour Bus

I had another opportunity to try out my "honest" sales skills as a college dean a few years ago. In the spring of 2006, the Admissions Office at Franklin & Marshall asked me to help out at our annual "A Closer Look" program, at which prospective applicants who have been accepted by the College in the spring of their senior year in high school are courted with the aim of enticing them to choose F&M over other schools. I have done many presentations for Admissions over the years, and they apparently thought I was an engaging and humorous speaker. This time, they asked me to be the tour guide on hourly afternoon bus tours around Lancaster for the prospective students and their parents.

I did my assigned duty on the first two tours—I pointed out, in my enthusiastic and occasionally humorous manner, some of the exciting things to do in Lancaster, Pennsylvania, and the many interesting historical sites of the city. As the afternoon wore on, I was growing pretty bored with repeating my spiel, so I decided to change the presentation for my final tour.

As the bus started to move, I announced: "Ladies and Gentlemen. I know that I am supposed to give you a tour of the City of Lancaster and point out some of the more exciting things to do and emphasize how historical the City is, but I'm not going to do that." The bus driver gave me an inquiring look. I was thinking he might be bored with my spiel, too.

"Instead, I'm going to give you free advice on where you should choose to go to college next fall." Everyone in the bus laughed.

"No, I'm serious. You think I'm going to tell you to go to Franklin & Marshall, but that's not true." They laughed harder. The driver even laughed.

"No, really! My daughters chose not to go here. One went to Connecticut College and the other went to Caltech. My wife and I both went to the University of Chicago. My wife was the first woman to teach philosophy at Colby College and we had a great experience there. And I taught at Middlebury, and have written a two-volume history of Middlebury College. I am actually an historian of higher education, and I know a great deal about liberal arts colleges. If you tell me which schools you are considering and a little about yourself, I promise to truthfully give you my opinion." There was a lot of derisive laughter on the bus. The driver looked uncertain.

"Look, people," I continued. "I know that you have been marketed to death for the past two years by hundreds of colleges. Everyone of them, including F&M, has told you all the wonderful things about their schools—the great faculty, the terrific facilities, the diverse student body, the amazing alumni—and I know you must be having a hard time choosing. Here's your chance to get one honest, informed, objective opinion before you make up your minds. Who wants to go first?" The bus was silent. The driver looked concerned.

Finally, a hand went up in the back of the bus. "I'm trying to decide between Colby and F&M."

"It's very cold in Waterville. Would that bother you?"

"No, I'm from upstate New York. I actually like winter."

"What do you want to study?"

"Not sure, but probably something in history or economics."

"It's close. Those departments at the two schools are about even, but you might want to pick Colby. Colby is just a little bit better than F&M. Who's next?" There was a brief dead silence on the bus, and then about 20 hands shot up along with shouts begging to be heard. The driver pulled over, stopped the bus, and stared at me."

"Keep driving," I told him. The bus pulled back into traffic, and the driver was shaking his head. I spent the rest of the tour trying to answer the numerous questions that the students and their parents threw at me. They had been dying for someone—anyone!—to tell them what to do. In most of the cases, I was honestly able to advise them to come to F&M, but even in some of the cases where I advised that they attend another school, they told me that they had been leaning that way, but because I had been honest, they were going to give F&M further consideration.

As we neared the end of the ride, I noted that there was only one girl and her father who had not asked me a question. She looked Greek or Italian.

"Young lady, you haven't said anything. What are YOUR options?"

"Well, I'm in at Swarthmore, Chicago, and F&M."

"What did we do—buy you? You are obviously very smart—Swarthmore and Chicago only take very smart people. If you are a little quirky, you might choose Swarthmore; otherwise, you've got to go to Chicago!" She looked sad, and I said to her: "Look, the tour's almost over, can I talk with you and your dad for a few minutes after everyone leaves the bus? What's your name?"

"Anatoli. Anatoli Karas. You can call me Toli." After everyone disembarked (and thanked me profusely), Toli and I chatted. I quickly determined she was probably just a bit too socially adept to enjoy Swarthmore thoroughly, so I spent nearly an hour trying to convince her and her father that she should go to the University of Chicago. It turned out, however, that she lived in Chicago, and she wanted to go away to school. She was going to pursue a pre-med curriculum, and because that is one of F&M's strengths, I finally tried to see if she might fit in here.

"What do you like to do outside the classroom?"

"I'm passionate about American musical theater."

"You're kidding!"

"No. I love to sing and dance in American musicals."

I told her about my passion for American musicals (see Chapter 3 below), and we started a great discussion. I told her about the opportunities to direct, produce, and act in American musicals with an all-student organization at F&M. Eventually, she came to F&M, even though all summer, I continued to urge her to change her mind and go to Chicago.

As in the case of my selling cars, I was unsuccessful in convincing her not to buy my product. As I look back on my sales career, this was really the last straw: There is no way that a person with my fear of misleading people can be a great salesman. I don't know how my father did it, but I'm not capable of following in his footsteps. Should I give sales one more chance now that I have retired? I don't think so! Unfortunately, "Being a Salesman" becomes the first item on The F**ket List.

Chapter 2:
WHY I'M NOT GOING TO BE
A CAB DRIVER

"What you doin' in this neighborhood, boy. I want a BLACK driver!"

"That's refreshing to hear, sir. You are the first person to say that to me in two summers on this job."

The Introduction

IN THE SUMMERS of 1966 and 1967, while working my way through college, I drove a taxi full time in Chicago. During those two summers, I wrecked several cabs, committed voyeuristic acts, aided and abetted in a kidnapping, and personally started the race riot of 1966, among many other things. Cab driving was one of the most exciting and unusual experiences of my life, and as I started to consider how I might spend my time in retirement, I couldn't help but think seriously about doing it again.

It all started back in April of 1966. I was sitting next to a friend of mine in the Social Science Reading Room of the Harper Library at the University of Chicago reading the school paper, *The Maroon*. I noticed an ad in the paper for cab drivers. The ad claimed you could earn $25 a day driving a cab—a princely sum in 1966. Since annual tuition at the U. of Chicago was $1,400 approximately, if I earned $125 a week for 12 weeks, I could earn the equivalent of a year's tuition. Today's tuition and fees at Chicago are over $40,000 (that doesn't even include room, board, books, etc.). Try making that as a cab driver in one summer! Anyway, I was about to turn the page, when my friend said, "You should really be a cab driver, David, you'd really enjoy it."

"What?" I hadn't really given the ad serious attention.

"My dad is president of the company, and he says people really can make $25 a day. Not only that, you're pretty much on your own—no boss hanging over you. And you can stop and eat when you want. It's kind of neat. And you get to meet interesting people. And..."

"Whoa! I'll probably end up working for my mother again this summer. I've been a clerk for the educational association where she is associate director for six consecutive summers now. It's air conditioned and pretty easy work."

"How much do you make?"

"Only about $70 a week." He had started me thinking. I had worked so many summers for my mother, it had become a habit. Maybe I should try something new. Of course, the last time I tried something different (selling encyclopedias), I'd landed in jail! Still, it sounded exciting, and I loved to drive.

When I told my mother, she did not object, except that she made me promise that I would only drive in the daylight hours.

I called the cab company, and they said that as soon as I turned 21 on June 17, I should take the qualifying test downtown at the Cook County offices, and show up at the garage—which was just a few blocks from our apartment building in South Shore—to start work. They said I could drive the daytime shift. I was ecstatic.

I took the test on my birthday. I had studied very hard for the test during which I would be asked where things were located in Chicago. It turned out to be a snap: 35 multiple choice questions, with three choices for each question. I can't recall the exact questions, but it was something like: "O'Hare Airport is on the northwest side of the city, the south side, or in Lake Michigan." You only had to get 17 of the 35 correct to pass. The only thing you couldn't do was erase an answer and change it. I got all 35 right, but was penalized one point because I had erased one answer. I asked why you couldn't erase, and the man said there had been a scandal a few years before in which certain people's answers were changed by the officials so that they could pass.

After I was told that I had passed, I immediately went down to the company's garage near my home to join the union—it was a union shop—and fill out the necessary forms, including one in which I swore I did not belong to any organizations that advocated the overthrow of the United States. I hated signing forms like that, on principle. Furthermore, those kind of laws never made any sense to me. After all, if you were a member of a really subversive organization, you'd sign the form anyway, and go about your business of overthrowing the United States or taking over the union or whatever you were supposed to subvert.

I was taught how to operate the meter in the cab and how to compute my day's earnings. It all seemed pretty easy.

I bought my cab hat, received my payroll number of 1324, and was told to report to work the next morning before 8:00 a.m. I couldn't wait.

The Door

I was so excited that I had trouble sleeping that night. When it was dawn I got up, had some breakfast, bought a morning Chicago *Sun-Times* out of a newspaper box on the corner, and walked the two blocks to the garage. It was 5:30 a.m. I saw the general manager, and I introduced myself to him. I later figured out that except for two older drivers, he and I were the only white people who worked in the garage. The other 150 or so drivers, mechanics, and clerks were all black. He wished me good luck, and gave me one piece of advice.

"As you probably know, the best cabs go to the drivers with the most seniority. Jack, the manager to whom you will report assigns the cabs—give him five, and you will have a better chance to get a decent cab, believe me."

"Thank you." I gave my payroll number to Jack, and—taking the advice of the general manager—slapped his hand a big five. Jack looked at me somewhat curiously, and then looked around for my cab assignment. He handed me the keys and my pay envelope. It was cab 1374. I went out into the parking lot to find it. I should have been disappointed, but I was too excited. Cab 1374 was a mess. It was old and not very clean inside. I spent some time neatening it up, and then I started the engine. I put it into gear, stepped on the gas, but it didn't move forward. I pushed the gas down a little further, and it inched forward. I thought that it just needed to be warmed up. I slowly drove it over to the garage on the other side of the street and asked if there were any calls. The telephone clerk gave me a slip that said to pick up Mrs. Jackson about three blocks away at the South Shore Country Club at the corner of 71st and South Shore Drive. My first passenger!

The cab seemed much less enthusiastic than I was about the prospect of picking up Mrs. Jackson. Maybe it knew that Jews or blacks were not allowed as members of the South Shore Country Club. Indeed, I could barely get it up to 30 miles per hour even though I floored it for three blocks. I turned into the Country Club driveway, past the sign that said "No Dogs Allowed." My mother always said that the sign really read "No Dogs or Jews Allowed." She always said this without any humor. I couldn't wait to tell her that I had been invited to the South Shore Country Club! I saw a woman waiting under the canopy at the front entrance, and stopped the cab in front of her. I jumped out of the cab, and ran around to open the back door for her.

"Mrs. Jackson?" She was startled, and stepped back.

"What's the problem, young man?" She was a middle-aged black woman carrying some cleaning supplies. Given the South Shore Country Club's membership policy, I assumed that she had been cleaning the place all night.

"I just wanted to open the door for you!" She looked at me as if I had escaped from an insane asylum.

"Are you a real cab driver? Cab drivers don't open doors in Chicago, sonny."

Undeterred, I dramatically pulled the door open. It creaked strangely, and fell off its hinges onto the driveway of the Country Club. I let go of it just in time, and it missed my right foot by about three inches.

"AHHH!" she shrieked. "Are you all right, fella?"

"Yes, ma'am. I'm sorry. Why don't you get in, and I'll put the door in after you. I don't want you to fall out."

She thought about it for a minute, and laughed. "No, put the door in first, and I'll sit next to the open door. I don't want you to lose the door again. I'll be okay."

I agreed, and with some effort, I put the door in the cab. I looked around to see if anybody noticed. I was afraid I had set back the chance of Jewish membership at the club ten years. I could see it now: the club's board of trustees was meeting to decide whether it should amend the rules and let in Jews.

"I know some good Jews," says one trustee, "and they would be a credit to the club."

"Yeah, but look what happens when we invite them here. Just the other morning, we allowed that Stameshkin to come in here with his cab, and what does he do? He aggressively opens the door—the show-off—and off it comes, right on our driveway."

"Did it leave a mark?"

"Jews are such show-offs."

"Aggressive!"

"Obnoxious!"

"Unpolished!"

"And they're all klutzes!"

"Well that Stameshkin is, anyway."

"Did Stameshkin really take the door off right in our driveway?"

"How terribly Jewish of him!"

"I vote against Jews in the club!"

"Me, too!"

"Then it's unanimous!"

I stood there looking in all directions. Nobody was around—after all, it was barely 6:00 a.m. So maybe nobody noticed. I finally got in the cab. "Where to, ma'am?"

"Take me home, please. 6832 Kenwood." I figured that it was about two miles away.

"Yes, ma'am. Would you like a look at the morning paper?" I handed her my *Sun-Times*. The car reluctantly moved forward.

"No, thank you, I'm too tired. I've been working all night. But I must say you are the first cab driver who ever offered me a newspaper."

"I bet I'm the first one who ever ripped a door off of his cab, too. And this is my first day on the job. I wonder if they'll fire me for this."

"Your first day? No wonder you're so polite! Well, I hope you keep it up—the world could use a little more politeness."

"Is it too windy back there with the door open?"

"I'll be fine. Are you going so slowly because the door is open—because you don't have to—I'll be fine."

"No, actually, I'm having trouble getting the car to accelerate. After I drop you off, I think I'll take the cab back to have the door repaired and have them look at the engine." We came to her house, and the meter read $1.00. She handed me a $1 bill and said that she never tipped, because she treated the cab as a necessity. I found out later that many poor and working-class people used cabs that way and rarely tipped. She wished me good luck and climbed through the empty door space. Cab 1374 hobbled back to the garage, as I prayed that the door wouldn't fall out of the back seat.

When I returned to the garage, I parked the cab out front. I told the assistant manager what happened.

"You opened the door for the lady and it fell off? In the driveway of the South Shore Country Club? You expect me to believe that?"

Many of the drivers were reporting to work, and they started laughing hysterically when they saw my cab and heard the assistant manager yelling at me.

"Hey, rookie, you notice your cab's missing something?"

"South Shore Country Club don't allow no three-doored cabs—didn't you know that, boy?"

"You ain't gonna get many tips if you lose your passengers!"

"Where did you find that cab, son?"

"Hey, Jerome, they finally got air conditioning in the new models!"

I tried to smile as I got back in the cab and drove the car into the garage so the mechanic could work on the car. He spent the next half hour wiring the door shut. He told me to make sure people entered through the other door. He said he didn't have time to work on the engine, but that the night-shift mechanic would fix it and the door for me when I brought it back that evening. He did set the carburetor up a bit, so it wouldn't be too bad. I thanked him. I tried the door, and it seemed secure. I started the engine, and it did sound a little better. Several drivers were yelling at me as I backed out of the garage.

"Boy, watch how you open that door next time!"

"If the other one falls off, just let 'em sit in the front with you."

What a way to start my first day.

Mr. Goldstein

After the mechanic fixed the door, the dispatcher told me to go to 77th and South Shore Drive to pick up Mr. Goldstein. He told me that Goldstein, even though he was well past retirement age, went downtown to his law office nearly every morning at this time (about 6:30 a.m.). The driver who regularly picked him up had quit a few days ago, and Goldstein would be looking for a regular driver. It was a tremendous advantage to get downtown early in the day. Not only was it an expensive ride (about $3.60), but the trip left the driver in downtown where there was a very good chance of getting a morning trip to the airport from one of the numerous downtown hotels (a magnificent $6.00 ride with the excellent possibility of another $6.00 trip back to downtown an hour or so later). Even if you missed the airport trip, there were numerous wealthy (tipping) passengers down-town trying to get to work or to early morning appointments from train stations or nearby apartments. Downtown was heaven, and a regular early morning trip downtown from the South Side was therefore heavily sought after. Since I was only a summer driver, they didn't want to give me such a gold mine, but I was the only one around at the time.

Our garage was just a few blocks from Goldstein's high-rise apartment building, but given my difficulty in getting the cab to accelerate and my first-day nervousness, it seemed to take a long time. When I arrived, I got out of the car and stood by the back door of the cab so that I could open it for him. Goldstein appeared, dapperly dressed, with a white summer suit, crim-son bow tie, hat and a gold-tipped cane. He must have been 75 at least.

"Good morning, Mr. Goldstein." He looked startled for a second.

"You're the driver?" he said in a haughty tone (everything Mr. Goldstein said was in that tone of superiority and mild disapproval). I opened up the door for him.

"Yessir." He got into the cab

"You're white." I ran around to my side and got in.

"Yessir. Would you like a look at the morning paper?"

"The morning paper?!" He looked at me incredulously. "You're not a real taxi driver. My partner, Harvey, put you up to this, right? Harvey's a great practical joker—the schmuck!"

"No sir. This is my first day on the job, and I apologize for the cab. It doesn't seem to be able to accelerate very quickly. But I will try to get you down to your office as fast as I can. It's at 8 N. LaSalle, right?"

"Harvey did this. You're not a real cab driver. First of all there aren't any white drivers at the South Shore garage. Second, no Chicago cab driver opens doors for passengers and offers them the *Sun-Times*. You're a fraud—go tell Harvey it was a great joke, but Meyer Goldstein is not yet so old that he can't spot a joker when he sees one."

"Really, sir, I am a driver." I handed my cab driver's license back to him.

"Stameshkin! You're Jewish?" He pronounced my name right the first time, which startled me.

"Yessir. All the Stameshkins are Jewish."

"Hah! That does it. Jews don't drive cabs—everybody knows that! You're a fraud!"

There was no way I was going to convince Mr. Goldstein, so I tried another tack. "It's just a summer job, sir. I will be a senior at the University of Chicago this fall, and I am earning the money I will need for law school or graduate school when I graduate next spring."

"University of Chicago? Let me get this straight. I am being driven to my office by a white, Jewish University of Chicago student who opens the door for me and offers me the *Sun-Times*? Do I have this right, Stameshkin?"

"Yessir. One of my friends at Chicago gave me the idea of driving a cab. His father is the president of the company."

"Burton Silverstein? I've done work for him and this company for years. He *does* have a boy at Chicago, come to think of it. So maybe you're on the level after all. Well, even if you're not, it's a good joke on Harvey's part. So let's talk, University boy. What do you know about politics?"

As I drove down the Outer Drive, with the sun rising over Lake Michigan on our right, we engaged in a spirited twenty-minute discussion about the Congressional primary election between Abner Mikva and Barrett O'Hara. I supported Mikva, a reform Democrat, and he supported the 20-year incumbent, O'Hara, who was a good Congressman, but who was in Mayor Richard Daley's camp (anathema to a young liberal such as myself). He was animated and passionate in his arguments (and treated my ideas with contempt), but he seemed to really enjoy the battle. When we reached his office, I raced around to open the door for him. He handed me a $5.00 bill for the $3.60 ride, and told me to keep the change. It was my first tip!

"Now, Stameshkin, you be ready tomorrow at 6:30 a.m., and I'll call for you at the garage. If Harvey set me up for this, I'll kill him. If not, I'll see you tomorrow. Tomorrow, we will talk about the Vietnam War. I suppose, that since you are a bright young naive know-it-all liberal, you oppose our involvement, Stameshkin. Is that right?

"Yessir, you're absolutely right about that one."

"Well, we'll see about *that* tomorrow." He started to walk away, but stopped suddenly. For the first time, he dropped his imperious tone, and asked, almost pleadingly: "Did Harvey set this up?" He grimaced and turned his back. "Ah, never mind. It's too late now. I hope I see you again, Stameshkin."

When I returned to the garage that evening and turned in my pay envelope, the manager asked me what I had said to Mr. Goldstein.

"Why?" I asked.

"He called from work, and asked if you were really an employee. I told him you were, and I asked if you had caused any problems. He said, no, and that he wanted you every day this summer. And if we didn't send you, he was going to use a different company."

"We just talked about politics, sir."

"Hmm. Well, okay, Stameshkin. We'll give you Goldstein for the summer."

"Thank you very much, sir."

I picked up Mr. Goldstein nearly every weekday morning that first summer. We talked about Vietnam, Israel, young people, taxes, Mayor Daley, the weather, and, particularly, race relations. His positions were fairly predictable after a while, but I thoroughly enjoyed our mornings together. I think he did, too. He would also talk about his dead wife, Molly (she drove him nuts when she was alive, but I could tell that he missed her terribly), his children and grandchildren (they never called), his relatives who died in the Holocaust, his synagogue (now that he was "old", the Rabbi never asked his advice anymore), his law career, and his business. I don't think I ever knew more about anyone (outside of my family) than I ended up knowing about Mr. Goldstein. He was so sure of himself (and full of himself) that he was not an easy person to like. He probably had few friends; in fact, aside from his law partners, he never mentioned friends. He was just a lonely old man—very successful, but very alone.

The next spring, I noticed in the obituaries that Mr. Goldstein had passed away. There was quite a write-up about him. He had been a very successful lawyer, a friend of Mayor Daley's, and was involved in the Democratic Party, his synagogue, and a variety of Chicago Jewish charities. But the obituary left out many important details that I would have added, particularly the great panama hats he wore, his haughty disregard for the opinions of others, his irascibility, and his racist views. Most important, the obituary did not even mention that Mr. Goldstein called for a taxi every weekday morning at 6:30, that his driver the past summer had been a white Jewish college student who argued fiercely with Mr. Goldstein about every political and social issue imaginable, and that this particular driver will never forget him.

The Fire

Actually, the rest of my first day on the job went quite well. Mr. Goldstein's ride placed me downtown, and I spent much of the day carrying well-off folks who tipped regularly (and sometimes even immoderately) between downtown and the Near North Side. The cab still wasn't accelerating very well, but nobody seemed to notice much.

My goal was to earn $25.00 each day. Since I was paid on a straight commission basis of 42.5% of the amount registered on the meter (after six months on the job, that figure was increased to 47.5%), and since I was making about $8 a day in tips, I needed to put about $40.00 on the meter to earn my $25. About 6:00 p.m., I had my $40.00, and I "deadheaded" (moved without a fare) back to the garage. I arrived at 6:45 p.m., parked my cab, quickly filled out the information on my pay envelope, and turned in my keys to the assistant manager. He glared at me.

"You've been out there nearly 13 hours, Stameshkin—that's the maximum—I don't want to see you out there any longer, do you understand?"

"Yessir. Oh, sir, the mechanic said that the night guy would fix the door that came off this morning, and figure out why the car doesn't accelerate very quickly."

"Don't worry, we'll have it ready." He was examining my envelope. "You got $40 today. That's a good day's work." He sounded almost friendly for the first time.

"I enjoyed it, sir."

He glared at me again. "Sure. Try doing it for a living, college boy. It's a lot different when it's not just a summer job."

I thought about what he had said all summer. He was right. I always figured that my days as a driver were numbered, and that I would probably have more lucrative and respectable employment in my future. That has indeed been the case. (Of course, some people may not think that college administrators are more "respectable" than cab drivers. In fact, I know a lot of faculty members who would have their doubts.) But I still have never had a job that gave me such opportunities to learn about people and about myself.

My second day as a cab driver was much more eventful than my first. I reported to work at 6:00 a.m. hoping that Mr. Goldstein would call for me to take him downtown. I presented Jack, the man who assigned the cabs, with my payroll number. He looked at me expectantly, so I once again slapped my hand against his. "Here's five," I said jauntily. Jack shook his head and gave me a somewhat pained look.

"We fixed 1374 last night," he mumbled. "The door works, and the car accelerates nicely. Let me know tonight how it works."

"Yessir. And thanks for fixing the cab."

"It's all yours, boy." Jack checked his watch. "Mr. Goldstein just called and wants you at 6:30. And remember, I want you in here no later than 6:45 tonight!"

"Right." The cab was in the garage rather than in the parking lot across the street. I started it up and put it in gear. The car shot forward before I could even touch my foot to the accelerator. I hit the brakes hard because I had to turn right as I exited the garage onto Exchange. The resulting screech as I made the turn almost on two wheels caught the attention of some of the drivers. I could hear them yelling and laughing at me as I finally managed to stop the cab in front of the garage.

"There goes that crazy rookie again."

"You mean the one who rips doors off his cab?"

"Yeah! Hey rookie, at that speed, you're going to book $100."

"If you can slow down to pick anybody up. Ha Ha Ha."

It had taken just about all my leg strength to stop the cab. They had fixed 1374 all right! I wanted to go back and get it repaired, but I was afraid I if I did, I would be unable to pick up Mr. Goldstein—and maybe I would lose him forever. So I let go of the brake and off went 1374 at breakneck speed.

After dropping Mr. Goldstein off downtown, I went to one of the several downtown train stations hoping to pick up a commuter coming off the early trains. That had worked really well the day before. At the Union Station, I picked up a quiet, pipe-smoking, tweedy fellow who asked me to take him over to the Northwestern University Downtown Campus where, I presumed, he was on the faculty. He was pleased to accept my newspaper, and happily read the financial news. Meanwhile, I tried to control my ancient cab, which was acting as if it had swallowed a barrel of Geritol. Most of the time I had to keep my foot on the brake, even when we were moving. When the car was stopped, if I put it into neutral, the engine revved so hard, it sounded like a jet that was about to take off.

About a block from the campus, which was just north of the downtown area near Lake Michigan, my passenger started sniffing the air.

"Young man, I think your cab is smoking."

I had noticed a good deal of smoke in the cab, but I assumed the financial news had excited the pipe-smoking professor into an unusual amount of puffing.

"Are you sure that the smoke is coming from the cab?" I asked, as we arrived at the campus entrance.

"(Cough) (Hack) No doubt at all (cough) (hack). You can let me off right here."

He paid me (with a nice tip), and wished me well. I drove for several blocks, and stopped the car opposite the Drake Hotel. The cab was filled with smoke, and, with the professor's pipe far removed from the scene, there was absolutely no doubt that the smoke was coming from 1374. I checked my instruction book to determine my course of action. On Page 6 ("What to Do in Case of a Breakdown"), it said that I should call in for help on my radio, and not to leave the cab for any reason. 1374 was one of the few cabs without a radio. I decided to find a phone and call my garage. I left the smoking cab and went into the Drake to use the pay phone. I told my manager that 1374 had broken down. He said he would send somebody out to tow me in, but that I should stay by the cab.

I returned to the cab, and pulled out my copy of F. Scott Fitzgerald's *This Side of Paradise*, which I had been reading while waiting for fares at cabstands. The smoke was getting pretty bad, and had attracted the attention of a number of the wealthy old ladies who lived in the Drake, as well as a policeman directing the early morning rush hour traffic at the nearest intersection. The ladies had their heads out the windows facing the street.

"Yoo hoo, sonny, your cab's on fire."

"You'd better get 'vay from 'dat cab, dear—it's going to explode."

I hadn't really given that possibility much thought. But I saw the cop coming running breathlessly up to me. "Get the hell out of here, he screamed. "That cab's gonna' blow. I've called the fire department."

I turned around, and now there were flames as well as smoke.

"But, officer, my manager said to stay with the cab. See, it says so right here in the book." I accidentally handed him my Fitzgerald novel instead of the regulations book.

"This Side of Paradise?! What the hell are you talking about? Let's get out of here." He threw the novel back at me, and almost dragged me across the street to the applause of the old ladies in the Drake. As we reached the other curb, the cab kind of exploded—not the fiery kind you see in the movies, but a pretty good one nonetheless. The ladies were thrilled and yelled their support to the policeman:

"Good work, officer."

"You saved dat crazy driver's life."

"See, Melba, I told you the police were good guys."

"'Dis is so exciting! Here come duh fire trucks."

And indeed, sirens blaring, two big fire trucks appeared, along with an ambulance. The firemen did a quick job of cooling down 1374, and the emergency medical guy checked me out and said I was all right. The policeman disagreed, and mumbled that I should be taken to the nutcase ward. Fortunately, I had taken my pay envelope and everything else of value out of the cab, because by the time the firemen had finished their work, old 1374 was nearly unrecognizable. Just in time, the company tow truck pulled up, and the driver started talking to me.

"Christ, what the hell did you do to the cab, buddy?"

"I didn't do anything. Somebody set the carburetor up too high, and I couldn't control it."

"The carburetor did all this? Come on, guy! Well, let's take it in." He towed it to the nearest garage, and I was eventually driven back to my garage.

Jack was all over me. "What the hell happened, Stameshkin?"

I tried to explain, but he was livid. "If you knew what the problem was, you should have reported the problem before you left the garage. In two days, you've just ruined one of the finest cabs in the fleet. Now go home, and report back tomorrow ready to work—safely!!"

The general manager had overhead all of this, and he stopped me as I left. "Jack's right, son. You've got to be more careful."

"Yessir. I guess I lose a chance at a day's pay?"

"Not completely, you'll receive some pay for the time you were disabled. By the way, you did give Jack five, didn't you?"

"Yessir, yesterday and today."

He looked puzzled. "Hmm. You should only have to do it once. Well, okay, see you tomorrow."

I left determined to be more careful in the future. I didn't go directly home. Instead, I took in a movie, and I arrived home at about 6:30 p.m. as if nothing unusual had happened. I wasn't going to tell my mother what happened: I was afraid that she would see some connection between my having been jailed in my second day of work as an encyclopedia salesman and nearly being blown up in my second day of cab driving. I didn't want her on the phone with my boss. I could imagine their conversation resembling too closely an earlier one between her and "Motivator" Jones.

"Now little mother, it was just a little smoke, that's all."

"Listen, you creep, you almost killed my son with your damn exploding cab."

"Now, mother, don't you think it's time to cut the apron strings?"

"Don't you think it's time to put some of your cabs in the junk heap instead of foisting them on innocent little boys?!"

I was determined not to return to work in my mother's office, and I went to bed promising myself to drive very safely the rest of the summer.

The Opera Singers

I reported for work on the third day, and Jack assigned me cab 1365. It was even older looking than 1374. I wondered what kinds of cabs Jack gave to those guys who *didn't* know they were supposed to "give him five." Oh, well, at least it started and moved in a fairly normal way. I tried all the doors—they worked. Maybe 1365 was an improvement, after all.

I took Mr. Goldstein downtown, made a couple of runs from the train stations during the early part of the morning rush, and ended up at the Palmer House (one of the finer downtown hotels). As usual, during the rush hour, there were no cabs waiting at the hotel cabstand, and the doorman was blowing his cab whistle furiously as a line of impatient people were waiting for a taxi. The doorman impatiently waved to me to wait as my passengers disembarked at the hotel, and he graciously opened the door for my next clients—a well-dressed elegant middle-aged couple. I was very pleased to see they had luggage, a very good sign that this could be an airport run—a lucrative $6.00 trip with the possibility of another $6.00 trip back within an hour or so (the cab line at O'Hare Airport was enormous; they had built a large separate parking lot in which we waited). The man tipped the doorman with a bill of some kind (those guys must have made a fortune in tips), and he closed the door.

"Where to, folks?"

"O'Hare. We're flying United," the man responded.

"Would you like a look at the paper?"

"No, thank you." He said it with more than a trace of condescension. They began a conversation about opera sopranos that they continued non-stop for the next 20 minutes. It was obvious that they wanted nothing more to do with the likes of an uncultured cab driver. I might as well not have been there.

This was rather disappointing. I had discovered in my first two days that the line, "Would you like a look at the paper" had usually elicited one of two excellent responses. Either the customer was somewhat taken aback at my politeness and asked me about myself (the conversation went on from there), or the passenger took the paper and started a discussion about something that was in the news. In a few cases, unfortunately, the rider either took the paper and read it quietly or refused the paper and looked out the window. Those people made life rather boring.

This was the first time I had a couple in my cab who wanted to talk, but not to me. Eavesdropping has its pleasures, but not on conversations about subjects of which I am ignorant. I knew next to nothing about opera. Still, I had few options, so I listened. (There were no glass dividers between the front and back seats of Chicago cabs in 1966). The woman was apparently a prima donna—a star of an opera company. She kept denigrating the voice of every female opera star she mentioned. The man apparently was a former singer and now was her agent, her husband, or something. He kept agreeing with her wholeheartedly, and he treated with ridicule or condescension all of the women the diva criticized.

As we approached O'Hare Airport, there were construction signs. I suddenly remembered that today work would begin on the new runway at O'Hare. In about 1,500 feet, our three-lane expressway would slow from 70 mph to about 10 mph in order to take four 90-degree turns that would take us around the construction and back onto the expressway into the airport. I was in the far left lane, going about 70. I hit my brake in order to take the first turn to the right. Nothing happened. I tried pumping the brake. Nothing happened again. The other cars were slowing down, but not 1365! I tried setting the emergency brake, with no success. In desperation, I pulled the emergency brake out hard in order to try it again, and it came out in my hand. Oh my God, just like the movies, I thought—I'm going to die! I quickly swung over onto the left shoulder so I wouldn't hit the car in front of me that had slowed down to make the first hard right. I just missed his fender. We were now only a few yards from the construction area. The workers had just finished setting up a long line of sawhorses with flashing lights on the roadway that would be under construction. I made one last futile try at the brakes, and yelled at my opera customers that I did not have any brakes, and that I was going to try and stop the car by crashing through the sawhorses up ahead.

"What did you say?" the man asked in disbelief.

"I can't stop," I screamed.

The woman immediately hit a high C that she sustained for the next 30 seconds. It nearly shattered my eardrum. The man pulled the woman close to him, and had a hysterical look on his face. He hit an E, just as I hit the first sawhorse at about 60 miles per hour. Actually, they sounded pretty good together—loud, but in nearly perfect harmony. KABOOM! I saw the pieces flying over the cab. The workmen, who had set the sawhorses up about 75 feet apart in neat rows, dove for cover. I hit the sawhorses one by one. KABOOM! KABOOM! KABOOM! Workmen were diving all over the construction area trying to stay out of my way. I was now driving parallel to the rest of the traffic, and I could see out of the corner of my eyes, the incredulous looks I was getting from the other drivers who were slowly moving to my right. KABOOM! KABOOM! I think I hit about 20 of them (the sawhorses, not the drivers). They slowed me down considerably. By the time I joined the traffic, I was down to 10 mph. All the time, I kept pumping the brake, hoping for a miracle. Nothing happened, until suddenly, when I had rejoined the traffic, the brakes started to work—almost as if nothing had been wrong. I pulled over to the side to compose myself. The opera couple had completed their duet, and were screaming at me. I was too concerned about the brakes and getting over to the side to give them much attention. I got out to see what kind of damage had been done to the front of the cab. The grillwork was a mess—it looked like I had been involved in a head-on crash. I pulled the remnants of one of the sawhorses out of what was left of the grillwork. Fortunately, the engine was not damaged and the radiator was intact—those old Checker cabs were built like tanks. I finally began listening to my passengers.

"You idiot. You could have gotten us killed!" he yelled.

"Let us out right here, you imbecile!" she screamed.

"Folks, I'm truly sorry. But I think the brakes are okay now. It would probably be safer for you to limp in with me—it's less than a mile to the United departure area, and I will go at a slow speed. If you get out here, you will be standing for a long time before I can get you another cab."

The man tried to convince his diva that I was probably right, but he was unsuccessful. She said they would walk. She opened the door, vaulted out of the cab, started singing something operatic in German, and marched toward the airport along the shoulder of the road. The poor man was forced to carry all the luggage as he trailed his angry soprano. I drove alongside and tried to convince them to come back in. She had on high heels, and was obviously very uncomfortable. After a few strides and more pleading from her impresario, she gave in and they stepped back into the cab.

"Would you like a look at the morning paper?" I asked.

"Just get us to the airport, you swine!" she screamed.

"Yes, ma'am."

"And we are going to report you to the airport police," he added.

"After the damage I caused back there, I don't think you will have to do that," I managed.

We made it up to the United departure area without further incident. Whatever was wrong with the brakes had apparently fixed itself. My passengers exited quickly and paid the fare. No tip. The most dangerous ride of my life, and I didn't even get a tip. Life isn't fair.

As I left the airport, I realized I either had to go to the airport security office or to my garage. In either case, Jack was going to find out. I was dead meat.

The Lucky Bounce

I deadheaded back to the garage, and again tried to explain to Jack what had happened. I must have looked so pitiful, begging him not to fire me, that I think he probably had to try hard not to laugh. But he managed to stay angry, and screamed at me to be more careful. He then assigned me another cab—1383—and wearily told me not to wreck it "if at all possible!"

Cab 1383 was the newest taxi I had driven up to that time (which wasn't saying much), and it seemed to perform well enough. I stopped about three blocks from the garage, and tried all the doors. I tested the brakes. Everything seemed to work. I spent much of the rest of the day driving on the South Side and particularly in Hyde Park, the area around the University of Chicago and the Museum of Science and Industry. Late in the afternoon, I headed for the large Hyde Park cabstand that the company maintained at the corner of 56th Street and Stony Island Avenue. The dispatcher there was usually pretty busy, as wealthy Hyde Parkers often took taxis to downtown. The stand also had a bathroom, and I needed to use it.

I pulled into the cabstand, parked my car, and set the emergency brake as I got out to use the facilities. The cabstand ran along 56th Street, which descended rather steeply as it moved west from Stony Island Avenue in order to fit beneath the Illinois Central tracks which ran right behind the cabstand. This meant that the rear of the cabstand was about 10 feet above the level of 56th Street. Cab drivers using the facilities parked perpendicular to 56th Street at the back edge of the lot before taking their place in line. That is why I set the emergency brake, for if the cab were to move forward just a few feet it would go over the edge of the lot and fall straight down about 10 feet to 56th Street below. As I was coming out of the bathroom, I heard this tremendous crash outside. I looked down to see what had happened. A cab had fallen off the ledge and was bouncing crazily along on 56th Street. I quickly congratulated myself on setting my parking brake, and looked around to see which unlucky driver had forgotten to do that. But everybody was looking at me.

"Hey, son, that yo' cab bouncing around down there?"

"You should always set the brake, boy!!"

"Hey, it's startin' to go down 56th—you better catch it!"

I looked again at the cab, and, indeed, it was mine—1383. It had luckily landed on its tires, bounced several times and had miraculously turned straight downhill, rolled down 56th Street under the IC tracks and was headed west. I took chase, with about ten drivers hooting and yelling encouragement from up on the cabstand. I was catching up with it, as it started to go up hill after going under the bridge. But after it stopped on the incline, it had begun to go back downhill again at a pretty good pace, and it was heading in reverse right for me. I turned around and started running back toward Stony Island with the cab in hot pursuit. I thought: what a way to die, to be run over by one's own cab. The drivers and the dispatcher (who had come out of his little office to watch the excitement) were doubled over with laughter at this point. After this chase scenario was repeated several times, the wonders of friction slowed the cab down sufficiently so that I was able to grab hold of the driver's door, get into the cab, and stop it.

Fortunately, the cab hadn't hit anybody or anything (except the street from 10 feet up), and seemed to be in decent shape. I took it back up to the cabstand, and, as everybody watched, I tried the emergency brake. It didn't work (no great surprise). The dispatcher told me to return the car to the garage to see if there had been any damage. I begged him to call the garage first and tell Jack that the accident hadn't been my fault—that I HAD set the emergency brake and it had not worked. The dispatcher said that while the accident might have broken the brake, I was probably telling the truth. He said he'd call.

I drove the cab back to the garage (it was nearly quitting time anyway), and the general manager, not Jack, was waiting for me with a very serious look on his face. I was prepared for the worst. He asked me to explain this latest of my misadventures. After I finished, he asked a surprising question.

"Son, are you sure you gave Jack five dollars twice?"

"Five dollars? What do you mean? You told me to give him five, and I slapped his hand five. You mean I was supposed to give him five *dollars*?"

The manager's expression changed from anger to a look of incredulity to a wide grin. Then he started laughing. He laughed so hard, I thought he was going to choke to death.

"Well, that explains a lot of things," he finally managed. "Now listen, Stameshkin. Tomorrow morning, give Jack $5.00 PLEASE!! And please be careful. I should fire you for wrecking three cabs in three days, but, first of all, we have received half a dozen phone calls from people complimenting you on your politeness and good driving over the past three days. Whatever you are doing out there with the passengers, keep it up. Secondly, you are bringing in good money—you are obviously working hard—when you aren't wrecking every cab in the fleet!"

I was terribly relieved. "Thank you, sir, for letting me stay on with the company, and I promise I will give Jack the $5.00."

I went home, and when my mother asked how things had gone that day, I merely responded that it was pretty much the same as the first two days—nothing too exciting. She smiled and served me a nice steak and salad dinner. I remember thinking that if I ever had kids, I would never believe anything my kids told *me* when *they* were 21.

The Affair

Around noon during my second week on the job, I picked up a lady and her five-year-old son on the North Side. She was about 30, and, except for the fact that she was obviously distraught, I remember her as being fairly attractive.

"Where to, ma'am?" I asked.

"How could they do this to me?" she cried.

"Ma'am?"

"My husband and my sister. I think they're having an affair!" She broke down almost completely.

"I'm sorry to hear that." The boy showed little interest in all of this. He kept looking around the cab with much curiosity. "Is there someplace I can take you?"

"I think they're screwing right now at her house. I have to know for sure. If they're really doing it, you know?"

"Right. Do you want me to take you there?"

"I guess."

"Mommy, what's screwing mean?" She ignored his question.

"Do you know her address?" I asked, anxious to get rolling.

"Know Helen's address?" The words came tumbling out. "My kid sister? Of course, I do. There were only the two of us. My mother miscarried three times after Helen was born—the third time she died—so it was just the two of us. I pretty much raised her after my mother passed away. I was eleven, Helen was six, and my father was on the road a lot. After all the meals I made for her, how could she do this to me?" There was a long pause, as she sat there obviously thinking about the past.

I was starting to worry that I would never get this lady out of my cab. "Ma'am, if you give me the address, I'll take you there."

"What if they're doing it, what should I do? I mean, I don't have a gun or anything. What should I do? Do you have a gun?"

"Who, me? Er...No, but I do have a copy of the *Sun-Times*, would you like to look at it?"

"No. Well, I guess I'll just play it by ear."

"Do you want to give me the address."

"2347 West Foster. Near the corner of Western."

"Right." I put down the flag, and took off. It was only about ten minutes away. As we drove, the woman became quiet, and looked sadly out the window, dabbing occasionally at her eyes with her hanky. The boy kept his eyes on the back of my head, and only occasionally peeked at his mother.

"I would have driven, but I didn't want them to see my car there. I thought maybe I could sneak a look in the window. Yes! That's it!"

"Ma'am?"

"Look, I want you to pull around in the back of the house in the alley."

"In the alley, ma'am?"

"Yes. There's a window in my sister's bedroom that over-looks the alley. It's on the first floor. I think if you stand up on the roof of the cab, you can get a good look in the room."

"Me?"

"Well, you don't expect me to look in there, do you? What if they're doing it? I don't think I could bear the sight. Haven't you heard of hysterical blindness where people become blind from seeing something horrible like their mother being raped or their parents dying in front of them? Would you like that to happen to me?"

"No, ma'am." I couldn't believe I was going to do this. I thought of telling her that I was afraid of heights and couldn't stand up on the cab. It's true—I can barely stand on a chair to change a light bulb without shaking. But, my phobias kind of paled in comparison with her problem. Still, I thought I would try to get out of it.

"I think it's against cab regulations, ma'am."

"Look, here's $5 if you do it!"

Well, that was about 20 per cent of my daily wages. That pretty much clinched it. I'd have to overcome my phobia. I thought what I was about to do was probably immoral. On the other hand, I rationalized, we were dealing with two pretty immoral people here: a sister and a husband who were cheating on her.

We pulled into the alley, and she directed me over to the side where we were right under the window. It was a row house, which was built hard on the alley. I suddenly had this fear that maybe the guy would have a gun. What a way to go. But the $5 gave me unaccustomed courage, and up I went. Fortunately, I could see everything on my knees—I never had to stand up—and I peeked in the window. It was a warm day, and the window was open. I guess they didn't have air conditioning. The drapes were partially closed but the breeze kept moving them so I could see occasionally. There were two nude people on the bed, one on top of the other. I watched for a while—fascinated—I don't think I had ever seen other people having sex before. (Reminder: this was 1966, when motion pictures and television weren't quite as explicit as they became later, and there was no Internet.) A muffled banging noise woke me from my voyeuristic reverie, and I realized that my passenger was pounding on the roof. I got down, and went back into the cab.

"So, what did you see?" she asked impatiently.

"Well, there were these two people, um…making love…"

"What's making love mean, mommy?" asked the boy.

"Did they look like this?" she implored, ignoring the boy, and showing me two photographs. I looked at them for a long time. There was little doubt in my mind that these were indeed the two people on the bed. Their athletic movements had revealed all aspects of their anatomy including their faces. They had exhibited different facial expressions than the innocent pictures I was examining, but it was her sister and her husband in that bed. Still, I didn't want to hurt her by telling her the truth. God knows what she would do.

"I'm not sure. I can't really tell positively."

"Well, certainly, the woman was my sister."

I looked at the picture again. "I can't tell because her back was to me most of the time."

"She was on top? God, he's never done that for me! Wait— did you see a tattoo on the woman's behind?"

"Yes, a flower of some kind…"

"A ROSE! Oh, my God, was it a rose?"

"It could have been. I'm not really very good at identifying flowers…"

She started crying again, and reached into her purse for some money. "What's the fare?"

"What do you mean she was on top, mommy?"

"It's $1.75, ma'am."

She handed me two bills. "Keep the change, and here's your $5.00. My God, people will do anything for money these days." She grabbed the boy and stalked out of the car.

"What does screwing mean, Mommy?"

"It's what your father is doing to me AND your Aunt Helen." She started to sob again as I pulled away.

That was the one and only time I ever climbed on the roof of my cab.

The Kidnapping

Driving on Sunday was always fun. The conflict between morality and immorality was brought home most strongly to me on that day. I often started the day by picking up high-class black hookers at various motels and driving them to their homes on the South Side. Occasionally, as a hooker exited the cab, a black family, dressed in their Sunday best, would get in and direct me to their African Methodist Episcopal Church.

While the kids looked so uncomfortable in their suits and ties or in their starched white dresses, the parents seemed so very proud to be taking their brood to church in a taxi. The most interesting moments occurred when the parents would eye the hooker exiting my cab. Sinners and saints. The hooker would wink at the father, the father would have trouble taking his eyes of the hooker, and the wife—with a look of contempt— would move everybody along very quickly into the cab.

The most memorable Sunday conflict between good and evil that I witnessed (all right, in which I was involved) took place about noon on the South Side during my second summer of driving. I had just dropped off a fare near 67th and Stony Island, when a black minister hailed me about 100 yards up the street. He was surrounded by three small children and a woman whom I took to be his wife. They were trying to restrain him from hailing me, and he kept trying to push them away. As I pulled up, I could hear them yelling at one another.

"Now, Henry, she's 18 years old, and she's got to find her own path."

"Get out of my way Louise. I'm going to bring her back from Satan. I'm her father, and it's my responsibility!"

"Henry, it's against the law. It would be kidnapping!"

"Daddy, please don't go, please don't go!"

"Children, let go! There's no stopping me!"

He tore himself loose, jumped in the cab, and shouted at me to get moving.

"Where to, sir?"

"What are YOU doin' here?"

"Sir, I'm driving the cab."

"No, I mean what's a white boy doing drivin' this cab?"

"Actually, there's a lot of white drivers in Chicago, sir. I'm about the only one in my garage, but..."

"No, I mean what you doin' in this neighborhood, boy. I want a BLACK driver!"

"That's refreshing to hear, sir. You are the first person to say that to me in two summers on this job."

He ignored me. "And since you are driving on the Lord's Day, I can also assume you are an atheist. Just when I needed a religious black man, I'm stuck with a white atheist. Lord give me help!"

"I'm not an atheist, sir. I'm Jewish. I go to my house of worship on Friday night or Saturday morning."

"White and Jewish. Oh, Lordy. Well, at least there's some hope of conversion for you."

"Oh, I don't mind being white, sir."

"What? Are you crazy, boy? I'm talking about you taking Jesus Christ as your personal savior. Anyway, take me to 63rd and Morgan. My little girl's being held prisoner there, and I've got to get her out."

"Prisoner, sir? Shouldn't we get the police involved?"

"Hah, big help they would be; they probably run the joint."

"What kind of joint is it, sir, and do you have the exact address?" I was poised to write this down on my pay envelope.

"She's in a...house of prostitution. My daughter. My beautiful Tina. And the whole congregation is talkin' about it. The Reverend Brown's own beautiful 18-year-old daughter—in a house of ill repute. Daughter of Satan. How could it happen? She was so lovely. She sang in my choir at church. She had a beautiful soprano voice. She had..." He broke down crying.

"Excuse me, sir, but you sound as if she were already dead."

"In the eyes of the Lord, she is, unless I can get her out of that dark hole of sin and back into the light of Jesus Christ. And I'm going to need your help. Yeah. Maybe the fact that you're a white boy will be a plus after all."

"Sir, I'm not allowed to enter such houses. It's against company policy."

"Forget your company policy, boy. You're answering to a higher law today. Listen, when we get to 63rd and Morgan, just park the car near the corner, and we'll go into that house, find her, and take her back with us."

"Wait a minute, let me get this straight. You want me to go into this place and help you find your daughter. Even if you find her, she may not want to go with you."

"That's where you come in, friend. We're going to carry her out if we have to, and I've got kind of a bad back, so I may need you to help me carry her."

"Doesn't this kind of constitute kidnapping, sir?"

"Poppycock, boy, you sound like my wife, Louise. Tina's my daughter, and I'll do with her as I like. She just a baby!"

"Eighteen-year-old girls are no babies, pardon my saying so sir. I've had some recent experience with them, and they can take care of themselves."

"Perhaps, but if they fall into the wrong path, it's the responsibility of the father to save them, and you are going to be Daddy's helper."

I wrote "63rd and Morgan" on the pay envelope, and reluctantly started to drive. We arrived at 63rd and Morgan and parked the cab. He told me to follow him, and we approached a large Victorian house a few buildings from the corner. The front door was open and he walked in. I gulped twice and followed him. A middle-aged African-American woman was sitting in her bathrobe drinking coffee at a table near the entrance and counting some money. She looked up when we walked in and smiled.

"I'm sorry, gentlemen, but we are closed on Sundays until 7:00 p.m. My girls need their sleep after Saturday nights."

"I'm not here on business, madam. I'm looking for my daughter, Tina Brown."

She smiled. "Tina? So you're her daddy. You must be very proud of her. She's the prettiest girl I've got. Very popular. You know how men like to be with the young, pretty ones."

"Where is she?"

"She's up on the second floor in Room 14. I'll go get her for you."

"That's all right, I can find it."

"No, it's our policy that the young ladies come down and escort their visitors to the room."

Reverend Brown had been pretty cool to this point, but he finally lost it. "I am NOT one of your VISITORS. I am her FATHER, and I am here to take her out of this SIN HOLE." He ran upstairs, with the madame in hot pursuit. I trailed behind.

"Sir, you cannot go up there," she yelled after him.

Reverend Brown pounded on Room 14. The door opened, and was immediately slammed shut.

"Open this door right now, Tina Mae Brown, or I'll bust it in."

"Daddy, you can't do this. I'm 18, and if I want to get some experience in life, that's my business."

"I'm taking you home young lady. Right now." And he stood back about five feet, took a running start, and crashed into the door. It broke open and Reverend Brown flew into Tina's room. She came running out screaming, dressed in little more than a bathrobe, and smashed right into me. We landed in a heap on the ground, as Reverend Brown recovered and came out into the hallway.

"Good work, boy," he yelled at me. "Now you take her legs and I'll take the arms." He was attempting to grab both of her wrists, and I was trying to disengage myself from Tina's very attractive and mostly uncovered young body.

A few of the other occupants of the floor had heard the door smashed in, and they had come out into the hall to see what was going on. They were startled, but a few of them retained their sense of humor.

"You don't need to break the doors down, fellas!"

"Yeah, and you don't have to hogtie the girl and take her to your place. You can do it right here in her room, honey, if you just wait a couple of hours."

"We only do kinky sex on Fridays and Saturdays, fellas."

"Angela, look, a white boy. When was the last time you had a white boy?"

"Last night, Jillian. Don't you remember that red-headed boy who came here about nine o'clock?"

"Oh yeah! But are you sure redheads are considered white?"

Meanwhile, we were struggling to get Tina down the stairs, and the madame was screaming at Reverend Brown that she was going to call the police.

"Go ahead, woman. I want to see you explain what all of these young women are doing in this place of sin."

Tina was kicking her legs trying to get loose and she managed to kick me in the groin. I groaned, and almost dropped her. One of her colleagues noticed my pain, and called out:

"Tina, honey, don't kick him THERE; he might want to come back later, and we need all the customers we can get."

We finally managed to carry Tina right out the door and into the cab. I was feeling nauseous from her kick, and I thought I was going to throw up, faint, or both.

"Are you going to fight us, girl, or will you just sit tight until we get home?" Reverend Brown asked her sternly.

Tina just nodded and started to cry quietly, and I gladly let go of her feet. She sat down in the back of the cab, and, after a few blocks, put her head on the Reverend's shoulder. He put his arm around her, and she cried most of the way back to the church. The Reverend whispered a few words into her ear at one point, and she smiled slightly.

"I'm sorry, Daddy, but I guess I just had to rebel a little. You've always been so strict, and I thought I'd never know nothin' 'bout the world. Well, now I know lots, some of which I wish I didn't know!" She started crying again, and her father comforted her.

When we arrived, Reverend Brown thanked me and gave me a nice tip. Tina smiled shyly at me, and asked if I was hurt badly. I lied that I wasn't. After they left the cab, I drove around for a while, trying to shake off my lingering nausea. I also found myself thinking about good and evil, and wondering whether the ends could ever justify the means.

The Riot

I have to admit that I have always been very disappointed that I was left out of the famous Chicago newspaperman Mike Royko's description of the 1966 Chicago riot in his best-selling book, *Boss*. After all, I had personally caused the billions of dollars of damage; and I was responsible for the thousands of extra hours that firemen, policemen, and national guardsmen had to work to keep things from even getting worse. As it was, much of the West Side was in anarchy and closed to the outside world for 23 terrible days that summer.

It all started on a very warm July 9. It had been extraordinarily hot for a week. By about 2:30 p.m., the temperature had reached 100 and the humidity was unbearable. I was downtown driving on Michigan Avenue in my non-air conditioned cab, when a young well-dressed black man with a briefcase hailed me. He jumped in and was surprised that I was white.

"Where to, sir."

"Umm. Well, it's on the West Side. Will you go to the West Side?" The West Side was a poor African-American ghetto that was considered the most crime-ridden part of Chicago.

"You give me the address, and I'll take you there. That's my job."

"Okay, if you say so. 4206 West Van Buren."

"Have some business out there?" I was kind of surprised that this conservatively dressed, well-spoken man wanted to go there.

"I'm an attorney, and I have a deposition to take. I'm sorry to bring you out there, but..."

"Hey, it's all right. Plenty hot, isn't it?"

"Hoo boy!"

"Would you like a look at the *Sun-Times*?" I handed him back the paper.

"Thank you." He seemed relieved to have an excuse not to talk to me. We rode quietly for the next fifteen minutes. About two blocks from his destination, we noticed that some kids had opened up a fire hydrant and were playing in the water that was streaming across the street.

"You'd better close your window," he warned me, as he rolled up his.

"Why?"

"They'll try to spray the water through your window—it's an old game they play."

The fireplug was on the passenger side of the street, so I would have had to stop the cab to lean over and roll up the window on that side of the cab. I was hot and tired, the kids near the hydrant were very small, and I doubted they had the strength or ability to pull it off. Moreover, I figured they wouldn't do it to a cab. So I rolled on, front windows open. Just as we were about to cross the stream of water, one of the little kids put his hand over the hydrant and directed the stream right into my passenger side window. His aim was perfect, and the water poured in on me. I was soaked, my pay envelope was soaked, and the front seat of the cab was filled with water. My passenger, of course, was saved from all of this because he had closed his window.

"Oh, I'm so sorry," he said. "But I did warn you."

"It's no problem," I managed, through gritted teeth. I was furious—as much at myself as the kids. I dropped the attorney off one block down the street. He paid his fare, gave me a nice tip, and again apologized for what happened. I wheeled the car around; I was going back to tell those kids a thing or two. I arrived at the site of the crime and parked my cab. I strode angrily toward the little kids who were by the hydrant, and all of a sudden I noticed that they weren't the only kids in the immediate vicinity. When they saw me coming, all of the kids lined up—they looked like organ pipes, with some pretty big pipes joining the little ones. One of the biggest pipes (at least 6'2") asked me if I had a problem. I quickly sized up the situation.

Here I was—a white Jewish guy, 170 pounds dripping wet (which, in fact, I was)—facing about ten black kids, ranging in age from 6 to 16. I was on their turf, and it was hot as hell. Nerves were frayed. I suddenly changed my demeanor, smiled, and said: "I just came by to thank you for giving my cab a wash and cooling me down."

"Alright, man," said the littlest pipe, smiling broadly. The other youngsters also smiled and laughed.

"See you later," I called, as I turned around and walked swiftly back to my cab. I drove a few blocks and spotted a police car parked on the street. I got out of the cab. There were two cops in the car—one white and one black. That was common in black residential areas.

"Excuse me, but I'd like to report something."

"Just get out of the shower, cabbie?" the white cop asked me, laughing.

"Kind of. Two blocks down Van Buren, some kids are spraying motorists with a fire hydrant as they go by. You might want to talk to them."

"Well, they're just hot," said the black cop. "But I guess we'd better turn off that hydrant."

"Thanks!" And I went off.

The next morning I almost fell over when I read in the paper that the West Side had exploded late that afternoon in one of the worst riots in the city's history. The immediate cause, the paper claimed, was the decision by the police to close some of the fire hydrants on the West Side because kids were using them to spray passing motorists.

Mike Royko passed away in 1997, and I remember at the time wishing I had written these stories earlier so that, just in case he published a revised edition of *Boss*, he would have known the true story of who caused those riots. After all, I was not even asking for the fifteen minutes of fame to which Andy Warhol says each of us is entitled; all I wanted was a footnote. Hey, what more could a historian desire?

The Last Passenger

During my two years as a cab driver, I spent quite a bit of time pretending to be somebody or something I was not. I often did this to ingratiate myself with customers and earn a larger tip; sometimes, I did it just because it was fun pretending. I have always enjoyed acting, and cab driving allowed me numerous opportunities to be on stage (see Chapter 3).

My most common form of pretense was to act as if I were a University of Chicago student working to save money so I could attend medical school, law school, or divinity school. That really wasn't far from the truth, since I was an undergraduate at Chicago planning to go to law school or graduate school in history. Still, I found early on that it made a big difference in tips—graduate school apparently was a little vague and it didn't have the high-ticket appeal of med school, law school, or even divinity school. If I picked up a nice Jewish passenger, it didn't take long for me to mention that I was entering Harvard Medical School or Harvard Law School in the fall, but that I wasn't sure if I had the funds to get through there. Huge tip. Or, if I had an upright WASP in the back seat, I just had to mention that I had been accepted to Harvard Divinity School, and the big tips rolled in.

That kind of acting was fairly simple. The whole enterprise became more challenging when my riders started mouthing racist and anti-Semitic sentiments. I needed carefully to mask my feelings if I wanted to be richly rewarded, and I was usually successful.

"Would you like to look at the newspaper, sir?"

"Sure. Thanks. Hey, look at this garbage about this Martin Luther King character. Who does he think he is coming to Chicago and telling us what to do? He's just getting our [N-word]s all upset. Them [N-word]s are gettin' as bad as them Kikes, you know?"

I gave him a full profile view of my prominent Jewish nose. "Is that right?"

"Sure! They want to take over everything from good white folks like us."

"Is that right?"

"Now you're a good Italian boy, right?"

"Sure, paison, Stameshkin—a great Sicilian name. Well, here's your stop. The meter says $1.50."

"All right, cousin, here's $2.50. You keep that $1.00 as a tip. It's good talking with somebody who understands what's going on in this country."

While I was almost universally successful in hiding my true thoughts until after the tip had been handed over, I had a few notable failures. For example, one day in the second summer, I picked up a well-dressed middle-aged man on LaSalle Street, Chicago's financial district. I tried my usual games with him, but he was too insistent, and, in the end, I lost the battle, i.e., I let my sentiments overwhelm my good judgment, and I identified myself before the tip was made.

"Stameshkin, what kind of name is that?"

"Long and difficult!"

"Ha! That's good! But really, now, it sounds Polish."

"Well, actually my father's side *is* from Cracow."

"You don't look very Polish, though."

"That's what people say."

"Actually, you almost look like you are of the Jewish persuasion, if you don't mind my saying."

"I don't mind."

"Well, are you Jewish?" I nodded affirmatively, and he went on in a very condescending tone. "Hey, you've got nothing to be ashamed of. You people are very successful in a lot of things. I bet you're going to school right now, and that you're going to be a doctor or lawyer, right?"

"You are absolutely right."

"And your people are all very smart."

"Without exception."

"And your people have a way with money, I can tell you that. I work in the financial district, and there is not another race like the Jews with the sense for financial acquisitiveness. And I like the way your people take care of your own and marry within your race. Are you serious with a young woman?"

"Yes. Here's her picture." I blew my cool and handed him a snapshot of my very blonde, very Scandinavian fiancee. He blanched.

"She's very pretty, but, she, um, doesn't look very, um..."

"Jewish? Oh, don't worry, she's converting."

"Converting?" He looked sick. No tip at all. Oh, well, it was worth the look on his face, I guess.

After two summers of driving, my last day at work finally arrived. I was getting ready to go out to Expo '67 in Montreal at the end of the summer with some of my friends, and then it was on to graduate school at the University of Wisconsin. The Woodrow Wilson Fellowship I had won would also support me the next summer, so this was probably the end of my cab driving for some time.

Nothing very unusual happened during the morning and afternoon of that Friday. But about 4:30 p.m., at the start of rush hour, I picked up a woman who wanted to go from the Gold Coast near Lake Michigan across town to visit her sister in a hospital on the West Side. She was about 65 years old, and, even though the temperature was nearly 90 degrees, she had on a fur coat. I asked if she had any particular route she preferred, but she left it up to me. The route I chose took us past the Cabrini-Green homes—a public housing project that has, at times, been considered one of the most crime-ridden in the nation. At that time, it had a slightly better reputation, but it was still a breeding ground of poverty, crime and hopelessness. As we went by the project, the lady looked away from the newspaper I had given her, and started a conversation.

"Look what we give the Colored, and they're still not happy. What more can we do for them?"

"Ma'am?"

"Those lovely apartments over there. We pay for them with our taxes, and they still riot and steal and complain."

I almost automatically entered into my "Is that right?" routine. But suddenly I remembered that this was my last day; indeed, given the time and the distance from my garage, she would be my last passenger. I planned to deadhead in as soon as I dropped her off. I had endured (for the sake of good tips) two summers of holding in my true feelings and emotions as literally hundreds of passengers mouthed racist, ultraconservative, and anti-Semitic crap in my cab. I could feel all my filters failing at once. It was finally time to give a little of it back!

"Excuse me, ma'am, but have you ever been in the projects?"

"Pardon me?"

"Have you ever actually been inside the buildings or have you seen them close up?"

"Well, heavens no. What would *I* be doing in such a place?"

"Well, I have. They smell like urine!!"

"Young man!!"

"That's right, urine. Do you know why? Because the elevators are always broken, and the little kids don't have time to climb the stairs to their apartments when they have to go."

"I don't want to listen to this."

"And drunks urinate on the stairs. And other men wait on the stairs and rape and rob the women as they climb up to their apartments."

"That's quite enough, young man!!"

"And racist pigs like you think it's this heavenly place. It's hell, lady! You and your Gold Coast friends wouldn't have the faintest idea of what it's like to live in such a place."

"I want you to stop this cab right now and let me out."

"Really? You want to be let out right here. Let me tell you something lady. There isn't another white person in the five-square-block area surrounding us. And cabs don't come in here very often either. But if you say so..."

I stopped the car and pulled over to the curb. She was obviously taken aback. "No, um, er, drive on," she said angrily. "But there's no reason to raise your voice. When I get to the hospital, I'm going to call your manager and complain. I'm writing down your name and cab number right now."

"Good, you do that lady. You're my last customer—ever—and I don't give a damn what you say to my boss. I've been listening to your kind for two summers without ever answering back. Now, YOU can listen. I never dreamed that the world was as racist as it is. I never knew that white people hated and feared blacks as much as they do. I knew it intellectually, but this has been different. It has been a real learning experience, lady. And I'll tell you something else I've learned this summer—something you will never learn because you are too old and too rich and too stupid."

"I don't have to listen to this."

"Yes, you do. And you will. What I've learned is really simple. There are some wonderful black people in the world and some real jerks. And the same goes for white people. It's probably true of every group of people—I just haven't had a chance to know many other kinds of people yet. I've sat in this seat for two summers listening to the likes of you making the same stupid, uneducated statements about Blacks, Jews, Puerto Ricans, and every other group. But you know what, lady? YOU DON'T KNOW S**T!!"

"You're hysterical! You should be locked up!"

"You're right! But this feels wonderful!" I turned around and gave her a gleeful glare that would have made Jack Nicholson proud. She cowered in the corner of the cab. When we arrived at the hospital, she threw some money in the front seat and literally ran out of the cab. She must have worked up quite a sweat running in her fur. She probably told her sister that a madman had picked her up, and she was lucky to have escaped with her life.

When I returned to the garage, I turned in my pay envelope, and reminded Jack that this was my last day. We shook hands.

"By the way, Stameshkin, what the hell did you say to this lady you took to the West Side Hospital about an hour ago? Damn, she was so upset—I never heard anything like that from one of *your* passengers. Usually they're all so happy that this nice polite college boy drove them..."

"Nice *white* polite college boy."

"Yeah! Ain't that the truth! But anyway, it's always real positive. So what's the story with this lady?"

"Jack, she was a real loony. Wearing a fur coat in this weather, do you believe that? She kept yelling at me the entire ride. I think she was about to go into the psycho ward. Anyway, she kept saying Cabrini-Green was a lovely place. A real nut case."

"Cabrini-Green lovely? Good grief, she must be crazy. Well that makes more sense. I knew nobody sane would ever complain about our fair-haired boy, Stameshkin." He laughed. "You've come a long way from the first couple days here when you just about put us out of business wrecking our cabs."

"Well, I just became more careful," I said with a bit of sarcasm, while I smacked his hand with mine, "and I learned all about giving someone five!"

"Yeah, right." He laughed hard for a while. "Good luck in school, now, and come back next summer."

"Well, we'll see what happens. I'll be up in Madison, you know."

"Oh, you'll come back. You like it too much."

But that's when it hit me: He was right—I loved the work, but I knew then that I would be reluctant to go back. I didn't think I could ever play the "Is that right?" tape again.

After much thought in recent days, I have again come to that same conclusion. In retirement, I'm going to try to maximize the amount of time I spend around people who provide me with positive interactions. The lady in the fur coat had heard the last word. Being a cab driver again? Add it to The F**ket List!

Chapter 3:
WHY I'M NOT GOING TO BE
A STAND-UP COMIC

"Jan, what's going on? Why are all these old people here?"

"Oh, it's Parents' Weekend, and a lot of us tried to get our parents to come up on Thursday night so they could come and hear your monologue this morning. Mine couldn't make it, but they said they would try to catch your show...er...class...next time."

"These are all PARENTS?"

"Yeah. We told them it was worth getting up here early..."

"These are PARENTS? And they are paying for an extra night at a motel to hear my stupid monologue? Oh my God!"

The Child Actor

M Y LOVE OF theater and comedy, particularly musical comedy, came from my mother. Born in 1913 in the Ukraine, she grew up in Worthington, Minnesota, until my grandfather moved his small grocery store to the Twin Cities. My mother was very smart. She skipped three years of school, entered the University of Minnesota in 1928 at the age of 15, and graduated four years later. She was a fine athlete and a terrific bridge player (she was a life master and played against Charles Goren and all the other greats in her day). She married my father, Sam, who was five years older, in 1933 at the height of the Great Depression. My father had finished high school, but, given the economic times (and the demands of his parents that he contribute money to the family), he went to work after briefly studying to be a dentist. My sister, Rocille, was born in 1937. My father fought in Greenland in World War II, but came home in 1944 a year before the war ended after contracting rheumatic fever. He recovered, and I was conceived that fall.

My father ("The Greatest Salesman in the World"—see Chapter 1) apparently suffered from some kind of bipolar disorder, and could not always work. For this reason, when I was not yet two years old, my mother left Rocille and me with our grandmother in 1947 to work in and around New York City for the United Jewish Appeal. Mother was a Zionist, a Socialist, and a supporter of the Labor Party in what would soon become Israel. She told me years later that, when she had worked in New York, she had been helping run guns to the Jews in Palestine as they prepared to defend themselves and/ or fight for a Jewish State. She told me that she was primarily a decoy in the constant cat and mouse game the UJA operatives played with American FBI agents who were trying to stop Americans from sending arms abroad. She would leave her hotel in the morning and would be followed by two FBI agents. She knew they were following her, and they knew that she knew it. As she left her hotel each morning, she would saucily hand her schedule to the agents, who were hiding behind their newspapers in the hotel lobby.

More relevant to this story, she also had a chance to attend countless Broadway shows (I assume the FBI agents went, too), and she fell in love with American musical theater. She saw the original cast of *South Pacific* and feasted on everything she could afford. When she returned to St. Paul, she was determined to pursue acting and musical theater. She was a terrific piano player and had a nice voice.

From the time I was very young, I remember always having this great need to entertain people and make people feel better. I got that from my father, who would do anything for anyone and particularly loved to entertain children with his antics. Any time he could bring a smile to someone's face or do someone a favor or make someone feel better, he was on top of the world! I have tried to emulate my father throughout my life, but I have never come close to his success at making people feel better.

So, influenced by a mother who was stage-struck and a father who only wanted to make other people happy, it is not surprising that I often thought I would end up in the entertainment business. I was a very verbal and expressive child, and, when I was seven, my mother arranged for me to acquire some acting experience through classes and performances at the Edyth Bush Little Theater in St. Paul. I won the part of

Price Charming in an abbreviated version of "Cinderella" and fell in love with the gorgeous eight-year-old girl playing the title role. Although I adored her blond curls (did all Jewish boys of my era yearn for blondes even at that age?), I think I primarily fell in love with her feet—God, she had the most lovely petite feet—I was actually trembling every time I put the slipper on her! A couple of times in rehearsals, I fumbled the shoe on purpose as I was trying it on her, just to have a chance to place her magical foot once more into the silver slipper. [Note: I am pleased to report that I did not develop a foot fetish, and other parts of women have attracted me much more as I grew older.]

Around this time, my mother, who had taken a job at the University of Minnesota, began to pursue a Master's degree in theater. She brought me to the University's radio station, KUOM, in response to the station's call for a child who could perform in several of their radio plays. After a successful audition, I was selected for the roles and performed in radio versions of *Turn of the Screw* and *Six Characters in Search of an Author*, among other shows. I couldn't really understand a lot of what was happening in these shows (probably a good thing!). As Miles in *Turn of the Screw*, I was involved with ghosts and I died under strange circumstances; and as the Son in *Six Characters in Search of an Author*, two of my siblings died at the end. I asked my mother about the shows, and she just told me to do everything the Director said. I apparently delivered my lines appropriately, because he and the rest of the staff seemed pretty happy with me. I came back several times to work there. They particularly enjoyed my sound effects— babies crying, cats and dogs, cattle, sheep—you name it, I did it. It cracked them up that some little kid could do that.

The Whistle

When I was old enough to get my first haircut, my father took me to a barbershop owned by Tim Howard and his father. As I mentioned in Chapter 1, my father sold combination storm and screen windows in St. Paul, and he had a large (and loyal) clientele in the small African-American community. Tim Howard and his father were very light-skinned African-Americans, and their barbershop was always filled with black men. I did not notice this fact until I was in third grade or so. It happened one day when Tim was cutting my hair, and, as usual, he and one of his patrons were in a loud (but friendly) argument about some political question. There was a sign in the shop prominently placed as you entered that declared in large letters, "DISCUSSION OF POLITICS AND RELIGION ENCOURAGED." Tim, in particular, would start such discussions with most of his customers. Often, the subject had to do with Civil Rights issues (this was the mid-1950s), and I innocently asked one day, when I was about nine years old, "Tim, why are you always talking about Negroes?" There was a sudden silence in the shop. My father (the only other white person present among the ten or so customers) turned red, and then everyone just cracked up laughing. "Look at me, son," Tim said. "Oh, my Gosh," I responded, "you're a Negro!" I started looking around the shop. "Wow, so is your Dad. Hey, everyone else in here is too, except for my Dad." "And you," said Tim. "Gee," I said, looking carefully at my skin and comparing it to his. "You're right!" Everyone gave my father a real going over after that!

Tim Howard was one of the leaders of the black community in St. Paul, and later honored as Baptist layman of the year for his efforts in re-locating blacks in St. Paul after the state ran the new interstate highway right through their very small neighborhood. It wasn't easy moving blacks into white neighborhoods in the late 1950s and early 1960s, but Tim had a wonderful way about him.

Tim also had the most amazing whistle I had ever heard. It was a trill, but it had an unusual resonance to it. To this day, I've never heard a more exciting trilled whistle. When I was about ten and had learned how to whistle, I asked him if he would teach me his special whistle. He said it was too hard to learn. Every month, I came back for my haircut and begged him to teach me. He kept saying that it was too difficult to learn, but I persisted. Finally, when I was about 12, he reluctantly agreed to show me how he did it, and I tried to imitate him, but I just didn't seem to get it. I practiced hard between haircuts, but it was no use. Every time I came in for my haircut, he would whistle his trill—it was so beautiful!—and I would try unsuccessfully to replicate it. He would show me again, and I would spend another month practicing. Finally, after months of trying, it just came to me one day. I was ecstatic! My family and friends thought the trill was incredibly cool! I couldn't wait to perform for Tim at my next haircut. When I proudly executed the whistle, I was disappointed at his reaction. He smiled a little, and said that I sounded good, but there was something in his eyes that made me wonder if he was really glad he had taught me.

I didn't think anything about this incident until the spring of 1979, some 20 years later. I was in a room in the student union of Dickinson College in Carlisle, Pennsylvania, recruiting students for The Harrisburg Urban Semester, a program I directed for Franklin & Marshall, Dickinson, Gettysburg, and Wilson Colleges. I was absent-mindedly whistling the trill while waiting for students to come in and talk with me about my program, when suddenly a very large and angry black custodian ran in the room with a mop raised like a weapon!

"Where did you learn that whistle!" he demanded. I was surprised and scared, but I quickly replied that my barber had taught me when I was a kid.

"Your barber was black?" he demanded menacingly. As he approached me, I was thinking that this custodian was actually was going to kill me! I wondered briefly whether it was possible to be beaten to death by a mop. I tried to rise out of my chair, but I was paralyzed by fear.

"Yes sir, he was black!" I thought that everyone was supposed to have a fight or flight response, and realized I wasn't able to do either one. Is this another Jewish problem, I agonized? What a wimp!

"He never should have taught you that!" he screamed.

"I won't do it again, I promise, I didn't mean anything by it, honest!"

He lowered the mop and seemed to get a hold of himself. "Do you know what that whistle is?"

"I think it's a trill between F and G—right?"

"What are you talking about, boy? That's the whistle of the Underground Railroad. No white people were ever supposed to know that whistle."

Once he said that, all of his anger seemed to escape, and he sat down with his head between his hands. I had an unopened can of Coke and I asked if he would like it. He took it, without saying anything, opened it, and took a long swig. I told him that I had actually done quite a bit of reading about the Underground Railroad and that I had taught African-American history at several schools. He looked at me inquisitively.

I went on. "Actually, there were a lot of white people involved in the Underground Railroad, and my guess was that some of them may have even been taught that whistle. In the Reconstruction Era and after, however, when whites were generally terrorizing blacks in the South and sections of the North, that whistle may have survived as a way for blacks to warn one another of trouble. At that time, the whistle became something only blacks would know and blacks would be careful not to teach it to whites. Do you think that's possible?"

He took another sip of the Coke. "I don't know, boy. I just know my grandfather told me it was the whistle of the Underground Railroad, and that only blacks know it. He tried to teach me, but I could never do it; you're the first person other than my grandpa who I have ever heard make that whistle. I miss my grandpa, even if he's been dead 40 years now." He finished the Coke and handed me the can. "Listen, I'm sorry I came at you like that."

"No, it's okay. I understand. I didn't mean to offend you, sir."

"I know that now. Tell me how your learned it. Tell me about your barber."

After I told me about Tim Howard, he asked: "Hey, just for my grandpa, could you whistle one more time?"

"Are you sure?"

"Yeah."

I smiled. "You won't come at me with that mop?"

He looked at the mop, now lying limply on the floor and laughed loudly. "You looked pretty scared, boy!"

"I WAS scared! Okay...I'll whistle it again, in your grandpa's memory. And, so for the first time, I whistled the beautiful trilled whistle of Tim Howard knowing its history and knowing why Tim Howard was so reluctant to teach me and so ambivalent in his response to my success in learning it.

For the past fifty-five years, I have entertained people with Tim Howard's whistle, but it has never been quite as joyful an experience for me since the black Dickinson custodian taught me the whistle's true origins. Still, it's one cool whistle!

The Opening

As I grew older, I turned into a smart-ass in school and the class clown. This charmed some teachers and drove others to distraction. I became a good storyteller, and regaled my friends with jokes. I used to watch comedians on television and dreamed of being on the Ed Sullivan, Sid Caesar or Ernie Kovacs shows some day. But I never had the guts to really go that route. It takes real courage to stand up in front of a group of strangers and try to make them laugh. So I picked another career path. I went to graduate school in history, and was hired for my first full-time college teaching job at Middlebury College in Vermont in 1972. When I was interviewed for the job, they asked if I was prepared (or at least willing) to teach a wide variety of courses in American history. I said enthusiastically that I was! I didn't lie, because I WAS willing, but not in the least prepared! In my two years teaching there, I taught six different courses (most of which I had never taught before). I was consistently just one long evening or weekend ahead of my students all of the time.

One of the courses I was asked to teach in the fall of 1972 was the History of American Education, a field of which I was particularly ignorant. In the late 1960s and early 1970s, a good number of Middlebury students wanted to become teachers, and the College had established a teaching certificate program; this course was one of the required classes in that program. So over 100 students, who were required to take my course, reported to class with droopy eyes at 8:00 a.m., Monday, Wednesday, and Friday. The first couple of meetings were a disaster. The great majority of students had quickly fallen asleep or tuned out by 8:05 a.m., and the rest looked as if they wished they could join them. I was mortified. I can't describe my unhappiness when I saw them going to sleep. This goes back to my strong desire to entertain people. I was boring these people to sleep. I had hoped to stimulate my students to want to learn more about American history. By Friday of the first week, I was seriously rethinking my career path.

Desperate, I decided to try and tell some jokes at the beginning of class to wake them up and possibly hold their attention for a little while at least. In essence, I decided to try to be a stand-up comedian. I was terribly nervous on the second Monday when I decided to give it a shot. I actually had some great material. My wife, Colleen, who was writing her doctoral dissertation for the Philosophy Department at the University of Michigan, stayed home during the days at our little rented farm house apartment just west of the College. We had a cat, Isaac, but she wanted a dog, too, to keep her company since I was on campus all day and sometimes at night. We chose an Irish Setter puppy, in part because the only kind of dog I had ever owned was Kelly, an Irish Setter that my family had in St. Paul from the time I was 5 until I turned 13 or so. We named our puppy Jacob (to go with Isaac, and leaving room for Abraham, who might be another addition of some kind to the family in the future). Irish Setters are so beautiful, but I had forgotten how stupid they are. Okay, maybe stupid is the wrong word—let's just say that they appear to have a really bad case of ADHD (Always Damn Happy Dogs). My wife had read that Irish Setters needed to be obedience trained young, or they would be out of control forever. Unfortunately, we discovered that the closest obedience class at that time was over an hour north of Middlebury up in the mountains.

We brought Jacob to the first class, which was located up a large hill in the middle of nowhere. We arrived, and a large number of pick-up trucks with gun racks were parked at the top of the hill where the trainer apparently lived and worked. We went into a barn-like structure and the instructor (who had the smartest Shetland Sheep Dog as her assistant) gave us a look when we walked in.

"You are bringing an Irish Setter to obedience training class?"

"Yes, ma'am. Is there a problem?"

"Well…it's just that it's hard to train an Irish Setter when they are this young."

"But my wife read that you have to train them young, or they'll never be controllable."

"Well…he seems pretty young."

"When is the best time to train them?"

She laughed. "Actually, right after they die! Just kidding!"

My wife didn't think this was very funny. "We'll work hard," she promised.

The instructor realized that my wife wasn't one to trifle with, and she let us enroll our dog. I looked around and noticed most of the other dog owners there were men who were training their dogs to hunt. They had arrived in their pick-up trucks with hunting rifles attached to the gun racks on the trucks. They were serious and laconic.

"That's a beautiful dog," I offered to the man next to me who had a large black dog of some breed that my wife would know (she annually watches the Westminster Dog Show and can tell you the breed of nearly every dog on the screen).

"Yup," he responded.

"Mine is an Irish Setter."

"Yup," he repeated.

"Are you training your dog to hunt?" I asked.

"Yup." Real Vermonters are very economical with their verbiage. Laconic doesn't even start to describe them.

After the first lesson, my wife worked Jacob day and night. She taught me how to help, too. My poor wife! That dog had the hardest time remembering from day to day what he had (supposedly) learned the day before. She started to buy books on obedience training. She did the same thing when she got pregnant five years later: we bought out bookstores for every book about childbirth; later, she purchased everything she could find on one-year-olds, two-year-olds, etc. I thought we would have to build extra rooms in our house—not for the kids, but for the books about children.

Anyway, because of my wife's diligence, Jacob began to figure it out. He began to "heel" on command, he would "sit," go into the "down" position when requested, and he even mastered the "down and stay." In this exercise, the owner commands the dog to go from the heel position to lie down next to the owner. The owner then says "stay" and walks forward a few feet and turns to face the dog. The dog must stay in the down position for three minutes. Seeing Jacob stay in any position for three minutes while awake was unbelievable. Jake was still having trouble remembering what he had learned the day before, so I suggested that we might smack him a little to get his attention at those moments, and that actually seemed to work somewhat. My wife is such a kind person with animals—she just couldn't smack him. So, I ended up doing a lot of the training as well.

After several lessons, the dogs have to pass their major test. They must demonstrate to the trainer that they can heel, sit, go down, and stay. Colleen told me that because Jacob had been particularly responsive to me in recent days, she wanted me to take him through the test. I was scared, but proud that she had placed her trust in me. We arrived, and all the pick-up trucks with the gun racks were parked at the top of the hill where the trainer lived and worked. We went into the barn-like structure. Most of the 25 or so owners and their dogs were already present. There was a palpable excitement in the air.

"Are you excited?" I asked the man with the large hunting dog.

"Yup," he exclaimed. I think he really was excited, although it's as hard to tell if a true Vermonter is excited as it is to tell if an Irish Setter is sad.

The test started out very well. Jacob demonstrated his hard earned ability to heel, sit, and go down. Then came the big test—the down and stay. Could Jacob, the Irish Setter, sit still for three minutes? He went down readily and obediently did not stand up or follow me when I walked away to face him. I was becoming very optimistic at the two-minute mark, when all of a sudden, for reasons that will forever be a mystery, Jake jumped up in the air and started barking hysterically. Naturally, every other dog in the place jumped up and started to bark hysterically, as well. The other 25 owners gave me looks that can only be described as deadly. After all, because of me (well, because of Jacob), every dog in the place had now failed the test. I quickly contemplated the possible penalty I might face if the owners headed for the gun racks on their pickup trucks. So, without a moment's pause, I ran out of the barn-like structure, pulling my barking dog and my distraught wife into our vehicle. I raced down the mountain, afraid of even looking in my rear-view mirror and seeing the inevitable parade of angry owners in their pickup trucks with the gun racks eager for retribution.

When I told my students in the 8:00 a.m. History of American Education class this story on that second Monday, they loved it, undoubtedly because anything was better than my lectures on the History of American Education. But the good news was that, after listening to my monologue, my students stayed awake for at least the next 30 minutes while I droned on about the History of American Education before they started to fall asleep again. I considered this a victory of sorts, and vowed to keep telling stories at the beginning of every class as long as I was able to salvage 30 minutes of their attention.

About halfway through the semester on a Friday morning at 7:55 a.m., as I approached the classroom to teach my History of American Education class, I could hear what sounded like hundreds of voices emerging from the room. Usually, the students were still half asleep when I walked in, and it was as quiet as a morgue. But today, there was a cacophony of sound coming from the room, and when I entered, I was shocked to see about 250 people crowded into the room. They were in the aisles, on window seats, and anywhere else they could find a place to stand or sit. Many of these people were old—I mean older—they seemed to be at least in their fifties. I checked my watch—maybe I missed my class, and this was someone else's class. I pinched myself to see if I was just dreaming, but

I recognized a number of my students, and I walked over to one of them who was sitting in the front row.

"Jan, what's going on? Why are all these old people here?"

"Oh, it's Parents' Weekend, Professor Stameshkin, and a lot of us tried to get our parents to come up on Thursday night so they could come and hear your monologue this morning. Mine couldn't make it, but they said they would try to catch your show...er...class...next time."

"These are all PARENTS?"

"Yeah. We told them it was worth getting up here early..."

"These are PARENTS? And they are paying for an extra night at a motel to hear my stupid monologue? Oh my God!"

"You're very funny, Mr. Stameshkin. Don't worry. They're going to love you."

"But, Jan, I'm 27 and all of you are 21 or 22—we're about the same age; my material is written for "our" generation. I'm not sure your parents are going to find this funny."

"Don't worry! The ones who wouldn't find it funny probably aren't here! Tell the story about your dog flunking out of obedience school. That one was priceless!"

"But you've already heard that one."

"So what? It's a great story!"

Jan was a pretty sharp kid, and I was grateful for her compliments and her optimism, but I still was almost paralyzed by fear. What if the parents didn't like the fact that their tuition dollars were being spent on a third-rate historian/fourth-rate stand-up comic, and they complained to the Dean? I needed this job! This was my career! And what kind of references would the Dean provide in the future? "David Stameshkin? He *seemed* like a bright young fellow, but he was fired because his monologues sucked. Parents complained. Admission numbers dropped precipitously, the school nearly had to close, etc., etc."

Well, I knew I had to begin the class because everything had become very quiet, and the audience...er...class...was looking very expectant. I took a deep breath, and decided I might as well give it everything I had. I came out from behind my podium and threw myself into the monologue describing (once again) the test that Jacob had failed. I was pleasantly surprised to notice that the parents were laughing even harder than their kids. This motivated me to become even more enthusiastic in my description of Jacob's failed "down and stay," and the dash down the mountain with the pickup trucks with the gun racks undoubtedly in hot pursuit.

During my entire monologue, Jan and several other students in the front row were making hand signals to me. They kept moving their right hands abruptly upwards from their laps in short quick motions. May I be immodest: I am a great charades player—I have even taught charades—but I had no idea what Jan and the others were trying to communicate. When I had completed the monologue, I received a standing ovation (even those who had been seated stood up), and I was glowing in the warmth of the moment. I followed this performance with one of my best lectures of the semester (I was improving as the semester went on), and, for the first time, all the students stayed awake for the entire class (okay, it's more likely they stayed awake because their parents were there, but still, I believe John Dewey's views on education have never been more cogently and enthusiastically presented!).

When the class was over, I received another ovation, and I quickly went over to Jan and the other students in the front row to ask them what they were trying to communicate with those hand gestures.

"Great monologue, Professor Stameshkin! It was even funnier the second time!" Jan enthused.

"Thanks, Jan. I appreciate your suggestion, but what was with all the hand gestures?"

"Oh, your fly has been wide open the whole class."

I took one quick look, and saw the awful truth. Not only was the fly open, but somehow a small portion of my jockey shorts were making an appearance—just in case the open fly itself wasn't noticed. I immediately turned my back to everyone and rectified the situation, but as soon as I turned back, the parents were lining up to meet me. One huge man came barreling down the aisle first with his much smaller wife and embarrassed son, Patrick, in tow. He was laughing uproariously and had a booming voice.

"Hi, Prof. We're Patrick's parents." He stared at my fly. "Oh, it looks like you finally figured out that your fly was down, eh?" He put his arm around me. "Son, that was the best OPENING I've ever seen in a class! Opening? Get it? Opening? Ha!!" I got it. "Thanks for opening up new vistas of knowledge for my boy, Patrick!" OPENING vistas? Get it?!" I smiled.

His wife managed to move in to say something. "Harold's got a great sense of humor, sir, I hope he didn't offend you."

"Oh, no. It's very...funny. It was awfully kind of you to come a day early and attend Patrick's classes."

"Oh, no." she said. "This is the only class we are going to. We're going back to the motel and get some rest. We took the red-eye to get here…"

"And we are going to fly back on Sunday," Harold interrupted. "FLY back? Get it, FLY back? Harold slapped me on the back, and, still laughing loudly, took his wife by the hand, and walked out. Patrick quietly apologized, begging forgiveness with his eyes. I smiled and threw him a "don't worry, I understand" look, and he seemed relieved as he ran after his parents.

As I met the other parents, I think I did a good job of covering my mortification; I smiled, thanked them for coming, and I accepted their plaudits, as well as the occasional remarks related to my fly. After class, I walked to my office, and I vowed two things: First, I would always check my fly before teaching a class. Second, I would NEVER become a stand-up comic. It's as if God had sent a message in the form of a "no-fly zone" on my ambitions to be a stand-up comedy. No FLY zone? Get it?! You got it.

That incident occurred 40 years ago, and since that time I have written nearly 30 shows, all of them musical parodies, many of which I have directed and in which I have performed; and, because of my reputation as being "entertaining," I have been asked to be the emcee at numerous events. After each of these occasions, people come up and congratulate me, and, without fail, someone says: "David, you missed your calling." I politely thank them for their kind words, smile, discreetly check my fly, and silently say to myself: "Stand-up comic? Forget it!"

As I contemplated retirement and considered carefully whether to give stand-up one more try, I quickly recalled my History of American Education class and the "fly disaster." I realized I still lacked the courage to really give stand-up a try, so I (sadly) add one more item to The F**ket List.

Chapter 4:
WHY I'M NOT GOING TO BE
A RABBI

I pounded on the locked X-ray Room door. "Hey! She's hav-
ing a contraction! Let me in! They said they would never sepa-
rate us. Damn it, let me in." I had been up all night, and I was
exhausted and angry. I fell to my knees and kept pounding on
the door. Then I heard a voice on the hospital intercom system.
"Good morning. It's 6:00 a.m., and this is Sister Joan with the
morning devotional. Let us pray."
Two nuns stopped behind me to pray, and one of them said
to me: "Young man, you don't have to kneel during the morning
devotional."
I stood up and turned on her. "I'm NOT kneeling." I screamed.
"I'm Jewish for God's sake, and we don't kneel! I'm trying to get
into the X-ray Room where my wife is having a back contrac-
tion, and they won't let me in even though they PROMISED
they would never separate us if I went to those damn Lamaze
classes. Huh! Huh! POOH!, Huh! Huh! POOH!, Huh! Huh!
POOH! See, I went to the classes!!" I turned back to the door,
and started shouting again, and pounding on the door with a

new fury. "LET ME IN!" The two nuns scurried off, obviously looking for an orderly to put a straightjacket on me and take me to the psychiatric ward on the fourth floor.

The Introduction

WHEN I WAS a young teenager, everyone thought I was going to be a Rabbi. At times, I guess I did, too, at least at those times when I didn't think I was going to be a stand-up comic, a Broadway star, or a super salesman like my Dad.

Although neither of my parents was terribly observant, they made sure I had a good Jewish education. And they were very proud to be Jewish. As I mentioned earlier, my mother spent time working for the United Jewish Appeal in New York City, during which she hinted that she may have helped run guns to the Jews in Palestine in the 1940s. I was proud of being Jewish, too. My parents always pointed out Jews who were mentioned in the news. It was very important that I knew that Einstein was Jewish, Jonas Salk was Jewish, Benny Goodman was Jewish, etc., etc. As a huge sports fan, I was particularly excited when I learned that Sandy Koufax was Jewish. When he declined to pitch in the World Series because it was Yom Kippur, I was very proud.

Of course, it wasn't all fun and games being Jewish in the 1950s. Indeed, in the 1950s and early 1960s, when my identity was being forged, I endured numerous rather memorable anti-Semitic experiences. In third grade, five of my best male friends made a circle around me on the playground and chanted, "David is a Jew, David is a Jew," until the teacher stopped them. In fourth grade, kids from the nearby Catholic parochial school used to scream "Kike" as they beat me up and stole my snack money on my way to Hebrew School nearly every Wednesday afternoon. My fifth grade teacher told me that she would not appoint me to the prestigious position of school crossing guard because I was Jewish. When I was in sixth grade, the golf pro at our public course would not promote me to Chief Caddy because I was Jewish. A girl I liked in junior high school told me her mother did not want her to go out with me any more because I was Jewish. There were many more incidents, but I think you get the idea. On top of that, the pictures and stories of the Holocaust began to find their way into my life in the 1950s, and, increasingly, in the 1960s. The horrific images of the gas chambers, and the survivors who looked like skeletons made me physically ill. People had been murdered just because they were Jewish—like me. Six million people. I thought a lot about my identity at that time.

One place I felt very comfortable was in my synagogue, Temple Mount Zion, an old St. Paul, Minnesota Reform congregation, founded in 1856 on the frontier, before Minnesota was even a state. It was the first synagogue founded in Minnesota. Many Easterners still don't believe that there actually are Jews in Minnesota, much less that they formed a congregation over 150 years ago with the required minyan, i.e., ten Jewish adults. They find it more believable when I tell them (apocryphally) it was established by a minyan of four Jews and six Native Americans. By the way, I have noticed that Minnesotans continue to confound Easterners, not only by harboring Jews, but also in the area of politics, by producing an unusually high number of "interesting" and influential politicians (considering how small the state is), such as Hubert Humphrey, Eugene McCarthy, Walter Mondale, Jesse Ventura,

Harold Stassen, Paul Wellstone, and, most recently, Michele Bachmann, Al Franken, and Tim Pawlenty.

Anyway, I really liked being at my synagogue. It was nice to know that there was a place where people didn't beat you up, or make fun of you because you were Jewish, or ask you strange questions all the time, or try to convert you. I loved learning Hebrew and celebrating the holidays. I went to a Jewish camp when I was ten, and that was really fun. I wasn't at all sure about the existence of God—that seemed pretty difficult to believe—but, by the time I was twelve, it was time to start preparing to be a Bar Mitzvah, and I was anxious to reach that objective, God or no God. My parents were told to send me to an elderly woman who would teach me how to chant my Haftarah and lead the service. But I also had to write a Bar Mitzvah speech, and that was supervised by our Rabbi, W. Gunther Plaut.

Is There a God?: The Red Marks

Rabbi Plaut (may he rest in peace—he died recently at the age of 99) scared the hell out of me and every other kid in our synagogue. He seemed like he was seven feet tall, and the adjective "imperious" doesn't begin to do him justice. He swept into the room as if God were actually accompanying him (probably walking behind him). His sermons—brilliant, stirring, and carefully crafted—were delivered as if each sentence had been carved in stone and brought down by Moses along with the Ten Commandments. Sometimes he was Jeremiah telling all of us that we were not doing nearly enough to bring justice to the world. Sometimes (especially on the High Holidays, when he had a full house, consisting mainly of people who only came to synagogue on the High Holidays) he glowered at us and reminded us that one could not be a good Jew without being an active part of the synagogue and the community. Hundreds of people walked out at the end of the services feeling enormous guilt as only good Jews can feel guilt (*pace* Catholics—you can repent any time you want, while Jews save it up for a whole year and spend the High Holidays expelling it; no wonder so many Jews suffer from irritable bowel syndrome!).

The initial meeting with Rabbi Plaut to discuss our Bar Mitzvah speeches was usually brief, but terrifying. We sat outside the closed door of his office waiting nervously for our turn to be scathingly criticized for our poorly constructed first drafts. We could imagine our unfortunate classmates being harangued in that imperious German-Jewish voice, and we shuddered, knowing we would be treated to a similar browbeating. Our classmates emerged from the office red-faced and near tears with their drafts covered with red ink. You could barely see some of the original typescripts because of the numerous corrections.

Finally, it was my turn. I came in and I saw he was looking over my paper. He was smiling! He briefly pointed to the chair facing him across a very large and well-ordered desk and went back to reading my draft. Finally, he sighed and handed it to me across the desk. "David, this is very good," he said kindly. "You have nothing to be ashamed of. " (This expression was one of the highest forms of praise given by Jews of my parents' and grandparents' generations!) "Think about the suggestion I have made at the end and make the few changes I have required. Otherwise, this is fine. You do not need to come back again." I looked at the paper. There were a few red marks noting one or two typos, a grammatical problem, and a recommendation in the form of a question posed at the very end about the theme of my talk—but that was it! I looked up at him in surprise, but he was already picking up the next student's paper.

"I can...go, Rabbi?"

"Yes.," he said offhandedly. "Please give my best to your mother."

"I...I...I will." I stood up quickly, still in disbelief over the small number of red marks on the paper. "Thank you for reading my draft and for giving me some things to think about."

He looked up, and after a short pause, he said: "David, you are a very smart boy, and you seem to enjoy Hebrew School. Have you ever considered being a Rabbi?" I slowly sat down again.

"A Rabbi...Rabbi?"

"Yes. Have you ever thought about that?"

Rabbi Plaut was really the only Rabbi I had ever known very well. He had been the Rabbi of our congregation since I was three years old. I actually couldn't imagine being like him—he spoke so confidently and he was amazingly erudite. My mother told me that he wrote books and articles. He commanded the complete attention of everyone in any room in which he was present. I just couldn't see myself ever earning that kind of respect. Furthermore, I always wanted to please everyone and make them feel better about themselves. Rabbi Plaut terrified all of us kids, and his High Holiday sermons made me (and I'm sure most of the congregation) feel guilty and inadequate. I didn't think I would want to do that. And, as I have mentioned, I had some serious doubts about the existence of God. I don't know how long it took me to answer him, but I finally blurted out, "I'm not really sure how you become a Rabbi, but I know I could never give the sermons you give or learn all the things you know or be respected the way you are, sir."

He laughed! I don't think I had ever seen him laugh before. He said he wanted to talk with me late in the afternoon on the Monday after my Bar Mitzvah, and I, of course, mumbled that I would be there.

I walked out of his office, and the other students waiting there immediately asked to see the draft, so they could commiserate with me about the red marks that covered all of these drafts. The student who was on his way to the door to the Rabbi's office, grabbed it from my hands, and he shook his head. "David, what is this? There are almost no red marks on the paper! I don't get it." The other students sitting there gathered around. They couldn't believe it either.

I didn't want them to think I was trying to show them up. "I guess he just hadn't spent much time on it for some reason," I lied.

"Oh, he told you to come back again?" one of them asked.

"Yes," I sort of lied again. "I need to go back." They all seemed relieved to hear that.

My Bar Mitzvah went very well. Rabbi Plaut did not conduct the service and was not present. We had a very large congregation, and there were usually two Bar Mitzvahs being conducted simultaneously every Saturday. The wealthy kids usually had theirs in the main sanctuary, because it held more people, and Rabbi Plaut officiated there; those of us who were less well off (and had fewer people attending) held our service in the smaller chapel, with another official conducting the service. I was told that I chanted my Haftarah beautifully; even the lady who taught me how to chant told me "I had nothing to be ashamed of."

The Director of the Religious School was present, and he must have told the Rabbi I did well, because when I went to see the Rabbi that next Monday afternoon, he said he had heard that I did an excellent job. He quickly came to the point. "David, I want you to lead afternoon services for the next month."

"Afternoon services?" I didn't even know there were weekday afternoon services!

"Several times a week, we have a minyan in the afternoon, mostly older congregants. I think they will get a kick out of you running the services."

"But Rabbi, I wouldn't know what to do!" I was pretty shaken.

"Don't worry. I want you to attend a couple of the services so you see how they work, and then Mr. Kieffer [my Hebrew School teacher] will work with you on any of the prayers which you find difficult. All right?"

There really wasn't a question mark at the end of his "all right." He gave me a measured look, and I knew I had no choice.

"Yes, Rabbi."

"Good! I will see you Wednesday at 4:25 p.m. here, and we'll walk over to the chapel."

Well, I learned the service and, after a week or two, I walked to the pulpit and introduced myself, and, much to the surprise of the old men in the chapel, I ran that service. At the end, they came up to me, smiling, and telling me—all five foot two of me—what a good job I had done.

"You have nothing to be ashamed of, boychik!"

"I was at your Bar Mitzvah service, so this is no surprise."

"Are you going to be here again next week?"

I was really shocked at how well everything had gone. I had already signed up to continue in Hebrew School (only one other boy joined me in 8th grade Hebrew School), and, over the next few years, even though I continued to have serious doubts about the existence of God, I began to think more seriously about becoming a Rabbi. After all, the praise was very important, but not as important as the missing red marks—those signified in particular that I had very little to be ashamed of.

Is There a God?: The Bowling Ball

My father was a wonderful man who would do anything for anyone, but he drove my mother to distraction. He was manic/depressive, and when he was manic, he would take strangers hundreds of miles to see relatives, and never tell my mother where he was or where he was going. He would give money to people in need or spend it on what she considered unnecessary things. He would be a terrific breadwinner for a while (The Greatest Salesman in the World), and then he would go into a deep depression and be unable to work at all. My mother finally couldn't take it anymore, and, for those reasons and others I will never completely understand, she told him to move out in early 1960. She was then informed that her job as Associate Director of the North Central Association of Colleges and Secondary Schools, an agency which accredited all the high schools and colleges in nineteen states in the Midwest, was moving from the University of Minnesota to the University of Chicago. She decided to move from St. Paul to Chicago in the fall of 1960 to keep her job. She sold our house, and she took me with her.

My father was very sad when we moved. He went out to Los Angeles to live with one of his brothers. He passed away in February 1962 of a heart attack. It was his third. At the funeral, my father's relatives screamed at my mother and told her that my father had died of a broken heart because she had thrown him out two years ago. I apparently fainted at that point, and I don't remember much after that.

About six days after we received word of my father's death, I received a letter from him. He told me in the letter that he was selling cars and doing well and hoping that my mother would take him back again. I was incredibly sad. I loved my Dad, and I couldn't believe that he was dead, at the relatively young age of 54. Such a kind and caring man, and he was dead while so many schmucks were alive. What kind of God would arrange things this way?! I went to see Rabbi Friedlander at my Chicago synagogue. He had Confirmed me in my first year in Chicago, but there were 45 kids in the class, and I never really had a chance to get to know him. He was very similar to Rabbi Plaut in that he was tall, handsome, brilliant, imposing, and incredibly confident in his German-Jewish manner.

"Rabbi," I asked. "How could this happen to such a good man? Why are there so many evil people still alive, and my father, who did so many good deeds daily, was dead. What kind of God would do that?" He told me that we cannot fathom God's will and that we have to keep our faith. I knew that many Jews had lost faith in God when they saw the pictures of the six million Jews who had died at the hands of Hitler—what kind of God would let such a thing happen—God must be dead! Now, I knew more personally how they felt. My faith was pretty much destroyed, and how could I—a non-believer—be a Rabbi if I could not comfort the family of a deceased without lying about my true feelings?

In June of 1963, a year and a few months after my father's death, I was about to graduate from the University of Chicago

Laboratory High School and enroll at the University of Chicago. The night before graduation, I was feeling very blue because my father would not be there at the ceremony. He was always so proud of my academic accomplishments, and I knew he would be beaming…if he were there. And I know he would have wanted to give me a present. So, I was mooning around the eighth floor apartment in which my mother and I lived along Lake Michigan in the South Shore neighborhood a few miles south of the University of Chicago feeling very sorry for myself.

My mother was very sensitive to my feelings, but she told me to stop moping around and to go clean out the small caged storage area we had in the basement of our building. Our storage area had not been disturbed much since we had moved in three years earlier, and, as I started to sift through the detritus, I came upon my father's old bowling ball bag. I opened it and there was my father's bowling ball. He taught me how to bowl when I was very young, and we bowled together a lot when I was a little kid in St. Paul. I loved to bowl, and I even joined a junior league when I was 13 and was one of the top bowlers.

I remember when my Dad purchased that ball in 1955 (I was ten) and had the holes drilled for his fat stubby fingers. The name "SAM" was engraved on the ball, along with the dates the holes were drilled. I knew my hand wouldn't fit in those holes because I inherited my hands from my mother's side of the family—slender, small fingers—and I remembered my father's fingers had been fatter and bigger. But, just for the heck of it, I stuck my fingers in the holes, and…they fit perfectly! I had never found a ball that fit my hand as well as my father's ball did. It was like a miracle. I sat down on top of the boxes in the storage area, and I realized that this was my father's high school graduation present to me. And I cried.

If miracles really happened, maybe God wasn't dead after all. But it would take more than one small miracle to convince me.

Is there a God?: The Red Scales

When my Mother and I moved to Chicago from St. Paul in the late summer of 1960, I was in shock. I had lived my whole life in St. Paul, and all my friends were there. Suddenly, I was going to have to attend a new high school where I would not know anyone. I was very nervous and upset. I went to get a haircut the week before school started at a barbershop near our new apartment in Chicago. The barber had only been cutting my hair for a minute or two, and he suddenly stopped.

"I've got some bad news for you, son. You've got ringworm."

"Ringworm?! Are you kidding?"

"No, son. You better go see a doctor." I had seen filmstrips in health class about ringworm, with bald kids wearing strange head coverings. That's the way I was going to enter my new high school?! No way! I wasn't going.

My mother made an appointment for me later that week with a dermatologist (it must have been easier to obtain appointments with specialists 50 years ago). The doctor examined me for a few minutes, and then gave me his prognosis.

"David, I have some good news and some bad news for you. Which do you want first?"

"I'll take the good news. I haven't had much lately."

"Okay. You don't have ringworm." I was so relieved!

"Thank God for that! Can you imagine me walking into my new high school early next week bald with my head covered? What's the bad news?"

"You have psoriasis."

"Psoriasis? What's that?"

"It's an inherited skin disease that often lies dormant until a very stressful event causes it to manifest itself for the first time. Have you had a major change in your life recently or been under great stress?"

"My parents have split, and I had to leave all my friends and move to Chicago. I guess those are pretty traumatic."

"I would say so. Let me tell you a little about psoriasis. It's not life threatening. There is no known cure, although radiation treatments can help reduce the symptoms. It usually gets worse as you grow older. So, although I know you are pleased right now that you don't have ringworm, actually psoriasis is a much more long-lasting and stubborn problem."

"So the disease won't just stay on my scalp?"

"No. It could attack you anywhere."

"My face?"

"Yes, that's quite common, especially near your scalp. It's likely also to appear on your elbows and knees. Just about anywhere, actually. I'm sorry."

Three years ago, my psoriasis celebrated its 50th anniversary inhabiting the exterior areas of my body and doing scab labor, so to speak. My psoriatic patches have been a consistent, though not a lethal, problem for me all these years, just as the good doctor said they would. But I will always be grateful to my psoriasis, and not just because it wasn't ringworm, but because it probably saved my life.

When I received my Selective Service draft number of 63 in 1967, I was sure I would end up in Vietnam eventually. I hated the war, but I wasn't going to lie and say I was a conscientious objector, because I knew there were wars in which I would fight. Some of my University of Chicago friends were looking for ways to flunk the draft physical, and they urged me to visit the Friends Meeting House on campus where a doctor would examine you to see if you might have some disease or condition that would keep you out of the army and out of Vietnam. I went there without much hope. The doctor was very caring and friendly (just what you would expect from the Society of Friends). He started to look me over, and asked me what the scaly patches were that covered significant parts of my body. I told him I had psoriasis. He smiled broadly, hugged me, and said: "Psoriasis? Son, you aren't going to have to kill anyone!"

"Are you kidding?"

"No! You are automatically 1-Y! [1-Y was a deferment category for those who had certain medical conditions.]

"But why? It just itches and looks awful. It wouldn't really get in the way of my fighting. Wait! Is it because there would be occasions where my platoon is hiding in the brush about to surprise the Viet Cong, and I would start scratching and the noise would alert the Cong and they would turn toward the bushes and RAT-A-TAT-TAT—my whole platoon is dead? Is that why, Doc?!"

"Actually—no." He was more than a little taken aback by my military ardor (and possibly my mediocre imitation of a machine gun). "It's just that people who have had psoriasis and then joined the United States Army have seen their symptoms worsen rapidly under the stressful conditions, and, since the Army cannot treat the disease, the soldiers with psoriasis have sued the Army for large amounts of money. The Army doesn't like to lose millions of dollars in lawsuits, so they will no longer draft guys with psoriasis."

"Oh, I see." I thought my rationale was much more interesting and dramatic, but I assumed he knew what he was talking about.

"Just get a note from your dermatologist, and show it to the doctor at your draft physical. You're not going to have to kill anyone!"

I thanked him, and I made an appointment with the same doctor who had diagnosed me with psoriasis eight years earlier. When I went to see him, I saw that he had patriotic signs in his office supporting the war in Vietnam. I came into his examining room and told him what I needed; he immediately refused to write a letter confirming my condition.

"Not a chance, David. You and your draft card-burning buddies need to defend our country just like we did in the Big War. Psoriasis has nothing to do with fighting!" And he stormed out of the examining room. After I left the doctor's office, I called my pacifist mother, who was still angry with me for not moving to Canada—she hated the war. "Let me have a crack at him," she begged. I told her to go ahead and try—what was there to lose? I was not sure exactly what she said to the good doctor, but one of his nurses called me a few days later to schedule another visit. When I arrived, the receptionist handed me the letter, and said: "Your mother must be a very persuasive individual, because this is the first such letter the doctor has signed."

"She is *very* persuasive," I said. Later I learned that my mother had threatened him with a variety of lawsuits (she used to work for a law firm and had started law school at one point), and he probably figured it wasn't worth the cost of fighting a suit and the risk that she might win! Anyway, for the first time, I was very grateful to my psoriasis, and gave many of the little scaly patches an extra loving scratch that night. I couldn't help but think that, given this little miracle, perhaps there was a God, and, if there were, God certainly worked in mysterious ways.

Is There a God?: The Birth

I entered the University of Chicago in the fall of 1963. Although the University had been coed for most of its existence, the ratio of men to women undergraduates at that time was 2.5:1, and the ratio in the graduate and professional schools was even larger. The dating prospects for male first year students were, therefore, rather dismal, particularly for those men (like me) who were not particularly attractive. I think I was one of the .5's in the 2.5. I did date a little my first year, and more my second year. At one point, in fact, I was going out with a girl to whom I was very attracted, but I lost out to a competitor who was much better looking and a lot more interesting (he definitely was NOT one of the .5 guys).

As I approached my junior year, I was determined to do better. I signed up to help with the move-in for the new first-years and asked to be assigned to Woodward Court, the new women's residence hall. I spent a long (and seemingly fruitless) day there carrying luggage of first-year women, but I was rewarded beyond my dreams late in the day when a cab pulled up and out came several students, including the most beautiful girl I had ever seen. She was blonde, slender, and extremely attractive. She was very tired, and she gladly accepted my offer to carry her bags to the fourth floor of Wallace House. I introduced myself and tried to make some small talk, but she was exhausted, so I figured I would follow up on my good deed by calling on her the next day. I did learn that her name was Colleen Miner and that she had been on a train from Seattle for the last 45 hours or so along with a bunch of kids from the Pacific Northwest.

I went back to my residence hall very excited, but certain that someone with her looks was way out of my league—the ".5 league." Still, I was 20 and overwhelmingly interested in succeeding in my quest to win this girl of my dreams. The next day, I called upon her, and she came down to the lobby of Woodward Court. She did not remember me at all. I was devastated.

"You carried my bags up the stairs yesterday?" She was looking me over.

"Yes, don't you remember? We talked about how you had decided to come to school here even though you had never seen the campus?"

"That is true. I remember getting out of the cab, but the rest of it is kind of a blur…I was so tired. I slept 12 hours last night. But, if you *did* help me, I hope I thanked you."

"Oh, you were wonderful. Don't worry. So, would you like to take a walk around the neighborhood. I went to high school at the University of Chicago Laboratory High School—it's just a block from here—and I know the neighborhood really well."

"Actually, I promised my roommate I'd take a walk with her, but maybe another time."

"Okay." I tried not to look too disappointed, but I was crushed. I thought I would try one more ploy. "You should stop by the Student Activities Fair tomorrow. You'll get a chance to see all the extracurricular activities you might want to sign up for. I'll be there. Maybe I'll see you."

"Okay. I have to go now, but thanks for calling." She left. All those bags I carried the day before, all for nothing, it appeared.

She did come to the Activities Fair, and, as one of the leaders of the Student Government, I was holding forth trying to impress a bunch of nerdy first year students with my patter about student government and campus politics. She smiled in the back of the group and, after listening for a while, moved on to the next table. As I continued my little talks during the next hour, I watched her move around the room. Several guys talked with her—one of them for quite a while (it was painful).

A few days later, my College House—Shorey House—had a little get-together, and one of the first-years in my House, Mike Rosenberg, had invited Colleen to come to the event. She came over with Mike to talk with me.

"I saw you at the Activities Fair. You were very funny."

"Thanks. Did you find anything you liked there...I mean, any activities that you might get involved in?"

She laughed. "Maybe. You guys have this lovely fireplace. Do you ever use it?"

"Yeah, we have fires sometimes. Why?"

"I thought it would be fun to build a fire and make s'mores. Do you have any chocolate bars, graham crackers, and marshmallows?"

"I don't think so, but we could go get some. I have a car. You want to come and help me? Mike, do you want to come along or do you want to work on getting the fire going?" Mike agreed to stay, and I took Colleen to the grocery store.

"Is this *your* car?"

"No, it's my mother's car. She only lives 10 minutes from here, so I get to borrow it a lot."

"Chicago is so flat. It's amazing. Seattle is just one hill after another. It's so beautiful."

"Chicago has some beautiful places, too. Lake Michigan is really lovely, and the downtown is something else. I'd love to take you on a car tour sometime, if you'd like. I'll show you the highest point in the City. There's quite a view from there."

"I'd like that. I like your enthusiasm about Chicago."

We returned to the party with the marshmallows, graham crackers, and chocolate bars. Mike and others had found some sticks, and Colleen, Mike, and I and others put some marshmallows on the sticks and started roasting them over the fire. I stuck mine deep into the fire and it was soon black as coals.

"What are you doing?!" she cried.

"I'm roasting my marshmallow." She grabbed the stick from me, and put another marshmallow on it.

"You're roasting it like a peasant. You don't stick it into the fire and burn the marshmallow. You keep it close to the flame but not in it, and you gradually turn the marshmallow until it becomes uniformly golden brown all around. See?"

She pulled the stick out and proudly showed me her perfectly roasted marshmallow. "Don't you ever go camping?"

"I don't think Jews camp, to be honest."

She laughed. "Well, that's about all my family does. I was almost born in a tent."

So not only was she out of my league, she had discovered that I couldn't even roast a marshmallow.

The next month or so was tremendously frustrating. I would ask Colleen to do things, and, once in a while, she would go out with me. But there were six to ten guys competing with me, and she would pull out her date book, whenever I asked her out.

"Sorry, I can't go with you this Friday. How about two weeks from this Saturday?"

Very frustrating.

But I didn't give up. I eventually took her on the car tour of Chicago, and she seemed to like my enthusiasm and sense of humor. I took her down the Outer Drive along Lake Michigan, and exited at 23rd Street and McCormick Place. The exit ramp in those days went up fairly steeply, and, at the top, I pointed out that we were at the highest point in Chicago.

She was somewhat incredulous. "You're telling me that the highest point in the City of Chicago is the top of an exit ramp off of an expressway?!"

"Well, it has to be some place!" Actually, I didn't really know where the highest point was, but you could always see a long way in every direction from that spot, so I *believed* it might be the highest point, anyway.

She thoroughly enjoyed the tour, and we went out several more times. Although I wasn't nearly as good looking as some of the other guys pursuing her, I did have a car and a good sense of humor, and both of those were helpful! By Thanksgiving, I had pretty much won her over.

In my senior year and her sophomore year, we became very serious, and one day in the spring of 1967, we met for lunch, as we often did, in the basement of one of the academic buildings where we sat on the floor together next to a soda vending machine. She brought me an egg salad sandwich on a bagel. I took one bite, and the egg salad, of course, went all over the place. I immediately proposed to her (we were already sitting on the floor, so it was easy to move into kneeling position), and she accepted. [Note: Thirty-one years later, we returned to that same spot when we were taking our younger daughter, Elizabeth, on a campus tour during her junior year of high school. The vending machine was still there. I knelt, and I told

Elizabeth that this was the exact spot where I proposed to her mother. Elizabeth, obviously embarrassed, disappeared down the hall as fast as I have ever seen her move.]

As Colleen and I became increasingly serious about our relationship, we had some pretty deep discussions regarding how we would handle religion if we married and had kids. We agreed, after much deliberation, that we should raise our kids "something" and not "lots of things" or "nothing." Colleen had been raised as a Congregationalist, but she told me that she had great difficulty accepting Jesus as the son of God. I had maintained my doubts about God since my father's death, but we both could see that I was much more attached to my Judaism than she was to her religious background.

She decided to explore conversion. She visited Rabbi Max Ticktin, a personable and highly regarded Hillel Rabbi at the University of Chicago. He asked Colleen what she was studying, and she said that she had discovered a love for philosophy and was hoping to major in it. They had great initial discussions about philosophy, and she began to study with Rabbi Ticktin with the objective of converting. They studied Maimonides and Buber, and, during her junior year (while I went off to graduate school at the University of Wisconsin), she completed her conversion studies.

She was apparently not the only person at the University of Chicago converting to Judaism at that time; indeed, two of her friends were also converting, and this was the basis of an unusual occurrence during her senior year. Colleen and several other Chicago seniors had been named finalists for a prestigious Danforth Fellowship that would pay for four years of graduate study. The Danforth Foundation (funded with money from Purina) had a religious affiliation with the Episcopal

Church at that time, so when the students were being interviewed, they were asked a question about their religious views.
The first student, Celeste Simmons, told the Danforth panel
that she had been raised Roman Catholic, but she had converted to Judaism to marry Bill Goldberg, a nice Jewish guy in
my College House. The second candidate, Dorothy McNamara,
told the panel that she had been raised Presbyterian, but she
had converted to Judaism to marry Henry Feldman, another
nice Jewish guy from Shorey House. The Committee was
highly amused. Colleen was next.

"So, young lady, what is your religious background?"

"Well my family belonged to a Congregational Church in
Seattle, but recently I converted…"

"…to Judaism," they interrupted her in unison, "so you
could marry a nice Jewish guy. Right?"

"Yes! How did you know?" Colleen was surprised.

"Well, it seems that all the women at the U. of C. are converting to marry Jewish men!"

Colleen told me later that she wouldn't be surprised if the
panel members imagined that some charismatic young Rabbi
was running around the U. of C. converting undergraduate
Christian women!

We were married in Colleen's home in Seattle on June
15, 1968, between Colleen's junior and senior years of college.
She was only 20, and I was two days shy of my 23rd birthday.
Colleen's parents were still in shock that she had converted.
They were willing to have a Rabbi marry us, but they didn't
want the wedding in a synagogue. We found a Rabbi willing
to come to the home to conduct the service, and everything
went well except that I missed the glass the first time when
I tried to break it with my foot at the end of the ceremony.

I had finished my course work for my Master's Degree in History at the University of Wisconsin-Madison that spring, but I was trying to complete my research for my Master's thesis that summer, so Colleen and I rented a place in Madison for June, July, and August. Colleen had managed to obtain a job as a camp counselor at a Jewish Summer Day Camp in Madison, and she had to report two days after our wedding. So, the day after our wedding (we spent our wedding night in an airport hotel opening gifts), we took an early flight to the Midwest so she could start work at the camp. On the third night of our marriage, Colleen was on an overnight with her campers. Honeymoon? We didn't have one. Any honeymoon would have to wait; in truth, we lacked the funds to go on a honeymoon anyway.

Counseling at the Jewish Day Camp proved to be a great opportunity (and a fun one at that) for Colleen to continue her Jewish education. Over the next eight years, as we both completed doctorates at the University of Michigan and took temporary teaching jobs at Middlebury College (me) and Westfield State College and Colby Colleges (Colleen), Colleen and I found ways to celebrate the Jewish holidays and maintain our Jewish identity.

In 1976, Colleen accepted a tenure-track job in the Philosophy Department at Millersville State College in Pennsylvania. We moved to nearby Lancaster, Pennsylvania, bought a house, and began to think seriously about starting a family. We discovered that there were very few women on the faculty, and that apparently a female faculty member had never taught while pregnant at Millersville, which had been until very recently a state teachers college. But we had been married nine years and Colleen was nearing 30. We both thought it was the right time to get pregnant.

Colleen was very certain of when she wanted to have the baby—right after she finished grading her final exams in the spring. That way, she could be with the baby for the entire summer before going back to teaching, and we would hire a nanny (day care was not really an option in 1977). We counted backwards nine months from that date in very early June 1977, and aimed to "get pregnant" in early September, 1976. It didn't work that time, but the next year, we hit it almost right on the button: Anne Miriam Stameshkin was conceived on Thursday, September 22, 1977 and was born on Wednesday, June 14, 1978. I remember vividly both the days of the conception and the birth.

In September of 1977, Colleen took her temperature often trying to figure out when she was ovulating. I was home writing my dissertation that fall, and she came home from teaching in the afternoon of September 22, 1977. She took her temperature, and yelled from our bedroom, "Get in here now! This is it!" I quickly complied, trying not to bow to the pressure of the moment or any type of performance anxiety!

Fortunately, everything went well, and she was right about the timing: a month or so later, she announced that we were pregnant. She carried the baby to term while teaching. Her Department Chair was not happy. "You will miss many classes because of morning sickness and other pregnancy issues," he whined. "This is not good." Colleen returned from this conversation, and told me that she was determined not to miss any classes. She said that if she had morning sickness, I was to bring her black coffee and graham crackers, which I did many times during the first three months of the pregnancy. This method worked, and she never missed one class the entire year.

On June 13, 1978, a few weeks after she turned in her last grades for the 1977-78 academic year, her water broke at 4:00 p.m., and we quickly drove five minutes to St. Joseph Hospital where she was admitted and moved to the obstetrics ward. She had convinced me to take a Lamaze childbirth class with her. We had been told that if I went through the class, I could stay with her at all times before and during the birth. St. Joseph had even converted one of their delivery rooms into a "birthing room," which was supposed to resemble a bedroom at home rather than the cold institutional delivery rooms in a hospital. It actually looked more like a Howard Johnson's motel room, but the idea was a good one. The catch was that you had to have completed the Lamaze course to qualify to use the birthing room. So, we attended a series of evening classes and learned, in particular, breathing techniques for dealing with the pain that accompanied contractions. The husband was supposed to keep his wife breathing the proper way during the contractions—huh! huh! POOH!, huh! Huh! POOH!, Huh! Huh! POOH!, etc. I was very skeptical, but, when her contractions started, it actually seemed to work somewhat. At least it made me feel useful.

Unfortunately, Colleen had painful three-minute contractions in the maternity ward for 14 hours—all night long—and finally, at 5:30 a.m., they measured her and announced that the baby just wasn't coming. They decided to take her for an x-ray to see what was happening. They wheeled her to the radiation area, and I, of course, came along. As we arrived, she was having a very painful back contraction, and we were Huh! Huh! POOHing when they wheeled her into the x-ray room, gently pushed me away, quickly closed the door, and locked it. I heard Colleen scream in pain.

I pounded on the locked door. "Hey! She's having a contraction! Let me in! They said they would never separate us. Damn it, let me in." I had been up all night, and I was exhausted and angry. I fell to my knees and kept pounding on the door. Then I heard a voice on the hospital intercom system.

"Good morning. It's 6:00 a.m., and this is Sister Joan with the morning devotional. Let us pray."

Two nuns stopped behind me to pray, and one of them said to me: "Young man, you don't have to kneel during the morning devotional."

I stood up and turned on her. "I'm NOT kneeling." I screamed. "I'm Jewish for God's sake, and we don't kneel! I'm trying to get into the x-ray room where my wife is having a back contraction, and they won't let me in even though they PROMISED they would never separate us if I went to those damn Lamaze classes. Huh! Huh! POOH!, Huh! Huh! POOH!, Huh! Huh! POOH! See, I went to the classes!! I've been up all night and I want to be with my wife." I turned back to the door, and started shouting again, and pounding on the door with a new fury. "LET ME IN!" The two nuns scurried off, most likely looking frantically for an orderly to put a straightjacket on me and take me to the psychiatric ward on the fourth floor.

At that moment, the door opened, and they wheeled her back down to the maternity ward, where she was the only woman in residence that night. They gave her Pitocin, a drug that induces labor, and told us it would take a while to work, if it worked at all. A few hours later, Colleen mumbled that she felt like she wanted to push. I remembered from the Lamaze class that "wanting to push" meant things were at the very end of the process. I ran out into the hall, and yelled, "SHE WANTS TO PUSH!" "SHE WANTS TO PUSH!" The nurse came up to us slowly and smiled pitifully at me. "We just measured her, and she's not even close."

"Well, could you measure her again?"

"Nurse, I want to push," Colleen moaned.

"Take it easy, honey, and we'll see what you measure." The nurse took the measurement, and yelled: "She's at 9! Oh my God, we need to get her into delivery right away." She ran out in the hall and told everyone to get ready. They all started scurrying around.

"Are we going into the birthing room now?" I asked. "Colleen really wanted to have the baby in there."

"I don't give a damn where I give birth, but I want to push NOW," she screamed.

"Okay, okay." I said.

"We don't even have time to prep her," the nurse said and they began wheeling her quickly down the hall into a regular delivery room. The nurse turned and threw four plastic garments at me—a gown and three others that looked like shoes. "If you want to be there during the delivery, put these on." As I was running down the hall chasing the gurney, I managed to put on the gown and two of the shoes, although one of them didn't fit very well. I put the third one on my head and raced into the operating room. Dr. Johnson was already there preparing to operate, as my wife kept crying that she had to push. The nurse and Dr. Johnson told me to stand at the end of the operating table behind my wife's head. Then they did a double take and started laughing hysterically while pointing at me.

"You've got a...a ...shoe...on your head," the nurse finally managed.

Well, THAT explained why only one of the two shoes fit. I exchanged the hat on my foot for the shoe on my head.

Meanwhile, Dr. Johnson was laughing so hard he could barely operate, and Colleen was in real pain.

I pleaded with him to stop laughing. "Doc, I've got all the stuff on the right body parts now—please help my wife!"

Dr. Johnson told me to relax and quickly moved into action; indeed, it wasn't long before my wife's pushing became more intense, and then the baby started to emerge. Dr. Johnson and the nurse urged her to keep pushing.

"Just a few more pushes, honey, you can do it," I cried. "Oh, wow, Colleen it's a girl!"

Watching it happen right in the room was an amazing experience. All the Lamaze movies and books about childbirth had not prepared me for seeing my wife give birth to our baby. It was another miracle. First the bowling ball, then the life-saving psoriasis, now a baby. Maybe there was a God. Of course, I hadn't slept in two days, so I knew that my judgment was not at its sharpest, but still…I gave it a lot of thought over the next few days.

In my excitement over the birth of my daughter, I was also saddened by the intense realization that neither of my parents would get to know my child. I had known that was the case, in an intellectual sense, ever since my mother had died six years earlier in 1972 at the age of 58. But now that we actually had a child, the fact that my daughter would never know her paternal grandparents became a very sad reality. We named our daughter, Anne, in memory of my mother (it's a tradition of Eastern European Jews—the Ashkenazi Jews—to name children after dead relatives). Watching my dynamic, athletic mother die over a nine-month period had been incredibly depressing. At the end, she had lost so much weight she looked like a Holocaust victim. I was an orphan at 26. It sucked.

After much thought, I determined that there was just too much unexplainable and apparently random evil in the world—from very significant events such as the Holocaust to very personal events such as my parents' early deaths—for me to be able to believe strongly in God, notwithstanding a miracle bowling ball, a life-saving skin disease, and a beautiful baby. So, how could I be a Rabbi?!

That feeling has continued for the 34 years following my older daughter's birth. I've tried to believe. I've been very active in my synagogue, in the Lancaster Jewish community, and with the Jewish students at Franklin & Marshall College where I worked from 1978-2012. I've been President of my congregation, Vice President of the local Federation, Hillel Advisor at Franklin & Marshall, a soloist in our congregational choir, a clarinetist in our Klezmer Band—the Chopped Liver River Band—and a substitute for both the Rabbi and our Cantorial Soloiost when they are out of town. I've officiated at funerals, named babies, conducted a Bat Mitzvah, and have done just about everything a Rabbi is allowed to do (except officiate at marriage ceremonies—you have to be a clergyman to do that). Our synagogue's Rabbi for the past 20 years, Jack Paskoff, is a real mensch and a wonderful, caring role model (and not imperious in the least). But still, I have never developed the deep and necessary spiritualism to be a Rabbi who could call upon a true belief in God to help people through the most troubling times.

I wish I believed. I wish I could be a Rabbi. But I can't. So, becoming a Rabbi reluctantly goes on The F**ket List. God (if there is one) forgive me for this decision, for this book, and particularly for the title. But, I hope You at least enjoyed some of the stories—I always thought that if there WAS a God, He /She would have to have one hell of a sense of humor!

AFTERWORD

The F**ket List (continued): A few things that are on many Bucket Lists …but NOT on mine!

1. Travel. I'm just happy being at home, to be honest. My wife, on the other hand, likes to travel, so I'm just guessing that I will be on the move.

2. Attending a Major League baseball game at every stadium in a single year (and similar goals for other professional sports). Although I am an avid sports fan, this would entail way too many motels, expensive hot dogs, inebriated fans, and travel (see #1 above).

3. Skydiving. I'm deathly afraid of heights (see "The Affair" in Chapter 2). I have significant trouble standing on a chair to change a light bulb, much less falling out of a plane 15,000 chair-lengths above the earth!

4. Climbing a mountain in Nepal (see #1 and #3 above).

5. Traveling to the Moon (are you kidding?).

The Bucket List

My Bucket List is relatively short, because I have already had a blessed life and experienced a lot of things that I had hoped to do. Still, here are a few items for the Bucket List:

1. Write a "real" musical comedy (not a parody spoof using someone else's music) and have it performed in a regional theater and/or on Broadway.

2. Publish at least one more historical monograph (I wrote a two-volume history of Middlebury College). I'm working on a biography of Joseph Battell (1839-1915), a Vermont philanthropist, town leader, early environmentalist, lover of

horses (and leading enemy of automobiles), newspaper editor, innkeeper, and amateur scientist.

3. Improve my piano skills (they are minimal at the moment), so I can play a Chopin waltz and a Scott Joplin rag.

4. Publish *The F**ket List* to enough acclaim that I would be invited by Jon Stewart to be a guest on *The Daily Show*, at which time I can tell him how much joy he has brought into my life (and the lives of millions of others who watch his show religiously).

While there is some hope for achieving #2 and #3, #1 is highly unlikely and #4 is really up to you! If you liked this book, please tell your friends and relatives to read it, too. If enough people read it, maybe (just maybe) #4 will happen! If not? Well, f**k it!